SHADES OF GRAY

Memoirs of a Prussian Saint
on the Eastern Front

SHADES OF GRAY

MEMOIRS OF A PRUSSIAN SAINT
ON THE EASTERN FRONT

————————————————

ARTHUR O. NAUJOKS, JR.

and

MICHAEL S. ELDREDGE

MILL CREEK PRESS

Salt Lake City, Utah

Library of Congress Control Number 2003114550
ISBN 0-974-01582-2 (acid-free paper)

Printed in the United States of America on acid-free paper
Mill Creek Press website address: www.millcreekpress.com
pfb32975
Second Printing, January 2005

For my parents

Wayne and Bonnie Eldredge

and

For Michelle

In Memoriam

Arthur O. Naujoks, Jr.
December 19, 1922
October 25, 2002

Traudy H. Naujoks
October 7, 1925
November 19, 1995

Table of Contents

Maps

SHADES OF GRAY

Memoirs of a Prussian Saint on the Eastern Front

INTRODUCTION
Michael S. Eldredge

I FIRST MET Art Naujoks in the summer of 1995. A mutual friend introduced us. He wanted me to hear this incredible story of a German submarine that surrendered at Portsmouth, New Hampshire in May 1945 with significant amounts of enriched uranium aboard. This story was eventually published in 2002 as *The Last Secrets of the Third Reich*.

As I sat in Art's study, I noticed a picture of a young man in a German army uniform. An Iron Cross medal hung on its frame. After much cajoling, I managed to get Art to talk about his experiences on the Eastern Front during World War II. He handed me a three-ring binder, which he said contained a memoir he had written a few years earlier.

For the next few days, I devoured his roughly written text. During my next visit, I told him that the story about the enriched uranium and the German submarine was fascinating, but I was much more interested in his memoirs. My reaction to his story was similar to that of others to whom I would recount this story over the next several years.

Art begrudgingly agreed to let me rewrite his memoirs and expand the text to include more peripheral information, which made the story even more intriguing. That process took more than seven years and included several enjoyable afternoons and evenings listening to Art describe his many experiences.

After one of the early visits, I contacted an old friend, Richard Roberts, at the History Department at Weber State University. An expert in military history, Dr. Roberts welcomed the opportunity to have Art visit a class. The classroom was packed on the scheduled day. At the end of the hour, the students would not let him leave. The experience was exhilarating for him, but also emotionally draining. As we drove back to Salt Lake City, he said to me, "Please, let's not do that again!" and we never did.

Understanding the depth of Art's emotions was an awakening for me. As I researched deeper and deeper into the details of his experiences, I realized how remarkable it was that he had survived at all, much less with any degree of stability.

During all of our discussions, he lost his composure only twice. The first time occurred as he recounted the fate of his childhood friends killed in the war. The second time, he was describing the day-by-day horror of trying to escape the Russian encirclement during the early months of 1943. At that point he shared an incredibly personal commitment he made to his Heavenly Father that he would do anything if he could just survive this horrible march on the *Rollbahn* behind enemy lines. That opportunity arose immediately after the war when he became a missionary serving his fellow church members in the desolation of postwar Germany.

Art's strong preference for writing in German, in spite of his excellent grasp of English, complicated the writing of these memoirs.

The stilted nature of his writing in English made his memoirs pretty stark - descriptive in one sense, but nowhere near the colorful descriptive narrative when he spoke. So my contribution to this book centered around recapturing his natural style.

It was a multi-stepped process. After an initial reading of his text, I did more background reading about the larger events going on around him. Based on that research, I made a list of many questions, which formed the basis of our following discussions.

For me, those discussions were the reward for my efforts. He talked endlessly of his youth and his various experiences while I took many notes. Next, I submitted the narrative I produced from those notes for his review. He would say, "You use words that I am not sure I have ever heard before!" After I explained what I was saying, he made me rewrite everything using words that he understood clearly. This was not a case of Art's being illiterate in English so much as it was a case of an arrogant lawyer writing with typical bombast. Art transformed me from a lawyer back into a historian.

From the beginning, Art was uncomfortable with the idea of publishing his memoirs. He was intensely humble and almost frightened at the thought of anyone taking notice of him personally. He believed no one cared about his story. More than once he tried to distract my attention away from his memoir and back to German submarines and enriched uranium. It was to no avail.

For me, this has been a labor of love. My life is so much better for having known Art. Since his passing in the fall of 2002, I have missed him terribly. Yet I am grateful for the impact he has had on my life and for the opportunity to assist in sharing his story. I believe it is a significant contribution to the historiography of church members at war, especially from his unique and subjective viewpoint.

Michael S. Eldredge
Salt Lake City, Utah
Memorial Day
May 31, 2004

FOREWORD

Arthur O. Naujoks, Jr.

HALF A CENTURY after the end of World War II, it seems a bit late to recall my experiences as a German soldier on the Eastern Front. Nevertheless, it is a significant understatement to say that these experiences have had a profound influence on my life over the past five decades. Somewhere between the two extremes, there is a balance; there is a middle ground that explains my need to recount events that, to me at least, are very painful.

More than a quarter of a million Germans, Hungarians, Romanians and Italians fought on the German Don Front at Stalingrad; less than five percent of them survived. Another 350,000 German soldiers died in Belarus in 1944, and these figures do not consider hundreds of thousands of other soldiers who died on the Eastern Front during the years between 1941 and 1945. On the Russian side, millions of people - soldiers, civilians, partisans - all died because of Germany's invasion of Russia.

No matter how history judges the German invasion of Russia, several of my countrymen and I obeyed the call to arms of the official government that ruled our country. Just as in America, the government conscripted German youth into military service under the law of the land. I did not have the foresight or understanding to review and judge the motives of German decision-makers in 1942. Nor did I have the option of refusing military service based on my conscience in a war which, like all wars, was morally wrong. No human being who has ever suffered the horrendous experience of war can deny that its course is unjust and disgusting to anyone with a sense of human decency.

I was born and raised a German, specifically a Prussian. I loved my country; I did not love Hitler. Just as many of my neighbors and friends may often criticize a president sitting in the White House, they, as I do, love their country. Similarly, I do not associate atrocities committed by individual Americans, such as those committed against Native Americans, black slaves or the innocent victims of My Lai, as an innate characteristic of Americans. The military campaigns in which I took part in France and the Soviet Union were not unlike the campaigns that had raged across Europe for thousands of years.

Like many Americans who lived in America during the fifties and sixties, I had been politically socialized to hate Communism during my youth in East Prussia. When I fought on the Don front, I was fighting Communism. But even then, I came to hate war for what it truly is.

Time has proved to be a true and just critic of the Nazi tyranny that was eventually responsible for the deaths of millions of people. Fifty years later, just as the Japanese were invited to stay away from the commemoration of the Pearl Harbor attack, Germans were also told that their presence at the Normandy memorial was equally unwanted. In another fifty years, those who still harbor hatred and anger over what happened in World War II will have passed from this life, and hopefully the scars will not be so visible. But while we still share this fragile world, it is my earnest belief that the time has long since passed for us to understand our history. No matter how cruel, unjust or immoral, the misfortunes of war and blame cannot be explained by the mere fact that one is German, Japanese, Jewish or black. We are all humans. Thus, we owe it to ourselves to be honest and forthright about our place in this world. We come here to experience and to learn and, hopefully, to become better through our trials and hardships.

As a Mormon, the paradoxical question of right versus wrong in World War II is for me personally even deeper, especially in light of the Articles of Faith which define our beliefs. Article 12 reads as follows:

> We believe in being subject to kings, presidents, rulers, and magistrates, in obeying, honoring, and sustaining the law.

Another Mormon scripture, found in the Doctrine and Covenants, Section 58, expands this doctrine. It states:

> Let no man break the laws of the land, for he that keepeth the laws of God hath no need to break the laws of the land. Wherefore, be subject to the powers that be, until he reigns whose right it is to reign, and subdues all enemies under his feet. Behold, the laws which ye have received from my hand are the laws of the church, and in this light ye shall hold them forth. Behold, here is wisdom.

The history of the Mormon Church is filled with stories of the sacrifice and valor of its members in upholding their faith and principles that we believe to be mandated by our Heavenly Father. Indeed, the stories of Mormons who resisted the Nazi regime in World War II are a source of both pride and sorrow for those who were affected by them. In some instances, Mormon youth lost their lives; in others, they survived. No matter what the outcome, however, we found ourselves subject to the same temporal and spiritual laws, which predicated the outcome.

It is not for me to say who obeyed in the proper manner and who did not. I do not expect that many others will ever be able to tread upon such holy ground in this life. I believe it is impossible to understand fully the obvious paradoxes that everyone experienced in the horrors of World War II. I believe that my experience has taught me great lessons, which were necessary for my understanding and progression in this life. If my experiences can in any way teach others as they progress through their trials in this earthly existence, then I have achieved my purpose in sharing these experiences.

> Arthur O. Naujoks, Jr.
> Salt Lake City, Utah
> September 2002

Editor's note: On Sunday, June 6, 2004, the sixtieth anniversary of D-Day, Germany was invited to participate in the ceremony. Chancellor Gerhard Schröder attended, and 'Deutschland Über Alles' was played. Germany had finally been forgiven.

CHAPTER 1

SURROUNDED

Stille Nacht, Hielige Nacht . . . [1]

THE GRUFF, OFF-KEY voice resonated deep within my soul as I sat quietly in our bunker. It was Christmas Eve, and as the year 1942 faded into history I wondered if it would prove to be my last. Our bunker sat atop a hill overlooking the Don River, which flowed in a southeasterly direction over the Russian steppes toward Stalingrad. On our right flank, a huge gap in the German Eastern Front lay open where the 3rd Romanian Army had once been entrenched. Just over a month earlier, the Red Army had blown through this weakest part of our lines and now encircled Stalingrad. My artillery group[2] was one of many in the German 6th Army desperately trying to hold our position.

Alles schlaft, einsam wacht . . .

All day we had behaved like children as we decorated our Christmas tree and prepared small gifts of candy and cookies sent from home. The cooks had worked hard to prepare a special dinner of noodles and goulash, with vanilla pudding for dessert. After dinner, as we lit the candles on our tree, the cold, gray surroundings of our bunker melted away. Memories of Christmases past with family and friends back home in Tilsit filled my thoughts. I shuddered at the possibility that I might never see any of them again.

nur das traute hoch heilige Paar . . .

My heart ached and tears flooded my eyes as more voices joined in; the irony of our circumstance was overwhelming. Feelings suppressed for months by the horrors of war burst from within. I quickly lost my composure. Others around me turned away to hide their grief. I had to get out of there; I needed to be alone.

Holder Knabe im lockigen Haar . . .

Outside, my tears froze before they hit the ground in the −40° Celsius temperature. From other bunkers I could hear the soft refrains of familiar carols drifting into an otherwise still night. Desperately I gazed into the heavens searching for answers that I knew would not be there. The Spirit seemed so close, yet so far away.

Schlaf in himmlischer Ruh . . .

The stars flashed brilliantly in the deep blue-black sky, just as they had for eons since God's second day of creation. The magnificence of the heavens above me was in sharp contrast with what lay below. Scattered in the snow were burned out hulks of tanks and the unrecovered remains of Russian and German soldiers frozen in their final earthly agony. The surreal scene of death and destruction was juxtaposed with an otherwise peaceful setting.

Schlaf in himmlischer Ruh!

All my life I had been taught that Communist Russians were godless and evil. The stillness of the night, however, belied this assumption, and was an indication that perhaps the Christmas Spirit had descended on both sides of the line. It occurred to me that the lifeless forms below me were the sons, brothers and fathers of loving family members back home - loved ones to whom their fate was still a mystery. These Russians had come here to defend their homeland, and even their blood would not fully consecrate this ground until the spring thaw. We had come to liberate them. But as this campaign wore on, it was becoming increasingly difficult to discern where tyranny ended and liberation began.

For the first time in my life, as I stood alone in the trenches of the Eastern Front, I was being forced to reconcile the deep spiritual beliefs that I had been taught since childhood. I could not balance them with the temporal reality of war, death, destruction and hatred. Duty, honor and country could no longer preserve the luster on my shield of faith.

Twenty-five years earlier, my father had stood in a similar situation in a trench on the Western Front in France. The rattle of gunfire and the rumble of tanks had interrupted his stillness as British "Tommies" overran his position. Luckily, he had survived and was interned as a prisoner for the duration of the war. As I contemplated my situation that night under the stars, however, I figured my odds of survival were infinitely less promising.

* * * * * *

A quote often attributed to George Santayana states that history is a pack of lies about things that never happened, written by people who weren't there. Sixty years after my experiences at Stalingrad, it is still difficult for me to comprehend what happened during late 1942 and early 1943. Now, when I hear these words, I understand more about what it means. I understand what is meant by history being written by the victors, and perhaps that is as it should be. To the victors go the spoils of war, and with that goes the right to record for posterity an account that befits a conquering hero, an army, a nation.

In the sixty years that have passed since I stood in those trenches on that Christmas Eve of 1942, I have found little published material that relates an accurate account of the experience of the Stalingrad front. Certainly, there were not many that survived the death march of trapped soldiers who eventually escaped through Russian lines near Sudzha in the early spring of 1943. Of the few who did escape, there is no way to determine how many of those died of wounds or exposure as a result of the march, or were killed later in the war. Thus, my subjective viewpoint is somewhat unique.

Over the years, I have recorded my memories in various notes and memoirs as they came to mind. I acknowledge that some of my recollections may be dim or inaccurate, but the account written here is to the best of my knowledge. In some instances, my memory has been refreshed by other historical writings. I take no issue with historians who have recounted the events in which I participated. I only add my recollections and experiences to what they have already written. Further, those who know me best - my family, my friends and neighbors from Tilsit, some of whom are neighbors today in Utah - will all agree that my view of the war, of Hitler, and of Fascism has not been conveniently acquired since the end of World War II. I was never one of Hitler's admirers, supporters, or willing executioners; neither were the vast majority of the Germans I knew.

* * * * * *

As I stood in the trenches that Christmas Eve, my thoughts were not crowded with political issues. I was not questioning why I was in Russia, or whether or not our cause was just. I was twenty years old and thought mostly about my family, my friends, and my future that night. War had turned out to be much different from the descriptions related by my father and grandfather.

This war was fierce, full of hate, and crowded with graphic images of death and destruction. It was one thing to look at a soldier as an enemy, ready to kill you at the first opportunity. It was quite another to hear a wounded Russian cry out in pain or sob for his wife or mother as he lay dying on the battlefield. The same was true for your comrades in arms, whom you knew personally. When they were wounded or lay dying, you ached for their pain and misfortune. You mourned for their family and loved ones as life flickered and passed away. You knew the names of their children, their parents, their wives and loved ones. What were they doing while you held their father, their brother, their husband or son, trying desperately to save him, to encourage him, to bring him back from Death's door? Perhaps they were gathered before a Yule log laughing and singing; or just enjoying the comfort and love of those present; or maybe praying for a soldier away at war, whose whereabouts or circumstances were unknown. By the time they learned of their soldier's death, he would have been gone for weeks, maybe months. Maybe they would never learn of his death, forced to live with the simple report that he was missing in action.

The conditions of war on the Russian front did not facilitate an accurate accounting of what was happening in every sector. Many soldiers on both sides were never accounted for. The circumstances of their demise left nothing to recognize. The vast number of soldiers killed was too large to comprehend. The battle for Stalingrad has been described as the most horrific battle of the twentieth century. It has been estimated that two million people died in that engagement, a number just smaller than the population of the entire State of Utah at the time of this writing.

* * * * * * *

If there is one thing I learned in the trenches of the Stalingrad front and on the ensuing escape march, it was the precious and sacred nature of life. Life had become seemingly worthless on the Eastern Front, especially for those on both sides who were so willing and eager to take it from another. I observed that some soldiers, both German and Russian, were particularly suited to war. They relished the opportunity to kill the enemy. They found great satisfaction in watching the enemy suffer and die: the more painful and frightful the death, the better. Their motivation was hatred. For them, the brief lull in fighting that Christmas Eve was an annoyance, a delay in the high stakes game of warfare.

For me, this was the basis of my struggle that night. It was the beginning of a great and profound learning experience for me; an epiphany of sorts. In watching the horrors of war, I had come to hate the inevitability of death. Death was so final, so senseless. From an individual perspective, a German soldier would aim his rifle and shoot a Russian soldier, who, mortally wounded, would suffer and die. The drama would be played out again when a Russian soldier would aim his rifle and shoot a German soldier, who likewise would suffer and die.

None of these people in this macabre death game ever knew each other. They had never spoken with each other. They had never quarreled. It was likely that none of them had ever committed a wrong against the other. They had simply been born into different cultures. They had grown up in those cultures with beliefs and doctrines that somehow instilled the thought that the death of a German soldier on one hand, or a Russian soldier on the other, would solve a basic political need. As you can see, I was failing as a good student of our famous Prussian General Carl von Clausewitz. Clausewitz wrote in *Vom Kriege*,

> Two motives lead men to War: instinctive hostility and hostile intention. In our definition of War, we have chosen as its characteristic the latter of these elements, because it is the most general. It is

impossible to conceive the passion of hatred of the
wildest description, bordering on mere instinct,
without combining with it the idea of a hostile
intention. On the other hand, hostile intentions
may often exist without being accompanied by any,
or at all events by any extreme, hostility of feeling.[3]

Some historians have argued that the beginning of World War I was
characteristic of a war that began with hostile intentions, but without
much instinctive hostility. Indeed, before the lights went out in Europe
in 1914, the countries that ultimately became enemies had somewhat
cordial relations and did not expect that the convoluted web of alliances
would draw them into such a horrid and disastrous war.

The war that I was experiencing in Russia, however, clearly included
"instinctive hostility:" it was downright hatred. I was beginning to
believe that Clausewitz might have been wrong. To me, it appeared at
times that both sides were driven purely by hatred. There were Germans
who put prisoners to death and devastated towns and countries. There
were Russians who responded in kind. These atrocities clearly fit the
Clausewitz definition, "rude acts of mere instincts," that were not
characteristic of civilized nations.[4]

I had become more personally involved in the war. I could not see
it as a "continuation of politics by other means." Political theory could
not account for the human side of war, the side of war that invariably
included human emotions and consequences. These emotions lay
outside the scientific theory and strategy undertaken by the political
leaders and generals who conducted the war as if it were a chess game

based on political theory. The Stalingrad front had clearly evolved far beyond theory into an inferno of hatred. The violent hurricane of war taught me to appreciate the sacred nature of a single human life. I learned this lesson through the unholy destruction of more than two million human lives, some of which I observed at the closest quarters.

* * * * * * *

As I stood in the trenches that Christmas Eve and looked out over the battlefield, and later as I trudged through death and destruction, I came to appreciate life. Each frozen corpse, each dying soldier begging for help, each comrade who pushed on in hope of survival, each of them was an individual. Each of them had a story to tell. Each of them had grown up among childhood friends, had played, laughed and danced at one time or another. Most of them had experienced love - the love of their parents, the love of wives and girlfriends. Each of them experienced things in life that brought them great joy. They experienced the beauty of poetry, art, reading a favorite author, sports, playing or listening to music, or just lying in the grass and watching the clouds float across the deep blue sky.

When that German or Russian soldier pointed his rifle at his enemy and pulled the trigger, a life would end in an instant, together with all the treasures and emotions that each individual soldier carried with him. A permanent hole would open in the lives of many other people and stay with them forever, until their own lives ended. Life became very precious to me. As time passed in our march to escape, each new day of fearsome death and destruction made life even more sacred.

* * * * * *

Millions of soldiers and civilians died in the battle for Stalingrad, most of whom have stories we will never know. How many Beethovens might have composed? How many Pushkins might have published? Our world suffered for this great misfortune.

I was fortunate and blessed to survive. I was lucky. So I now tell my story. I tell my story of whom I am, how I came to be a Prussian, how I came to be a soldier in the Reich. I tell of fighting in a place I did not want to be, for a leader and a cause for which I had no respect. I tell my story for those whose lives are now forgotten. I remember them and wish they were here to tell their own stories.

CHAPTER 2
A YOUTH IN EAST PRUSSIA

I WAS BORN in East Prussia, just north of the Memel River, on Tuesday evening, December 19, 1922. Snow had been falling all day, covering the landscape with fluffy white flakes that billowed around my father's boots as he tramped to the stable late in the afternoon. Sensing the time had come for my arrival, father decided to harness his mare Lotte to the sled and fetch the midwife. With the same care that he always took as he worked, father soon had Lotte hitched up and trotting down the snow-packed road at a fast clip. On his right were the dark, primeval forests, the sacred *Alcas*, which served as temples for the ancient Baltic people. To his left, fallow fields and meadows lay under a glittering blanket of white.

The trip to the next village was not long, and by nightfall father and the midwife returned to the farmhouse. Grandma and neighbor ladies were preparing clean towels and warm blankets for my delivery. Father assumed the traditional role of a husband in waiting, sitting by the fire in quiet contemplation. Years later he shared with me his memories of that night. They were memories of hopes and dreams he held for a son who would one day acquire land and farm nearby; a son he would love, a son he would teach, a son he would be proud of.

Our farmhouse was small, with modest furnishings. Like thousands of other farms north of the Memel River, it belied the passage of time.

Sitting in our farmhouse, you couldn't tell whether it was the 20th century or the 18th century. Utensils were the same, furniture and fixtures the same; ruggedness and warmth, still the same. Except for a rare photograph, a recent book, or a newspaper, time had no identity. On this night, as on a thousand other nights on a thousand other farms, a new generation was arriving to carry on the traditions of its fathers, to improve where improvement was needed, but mostly just to carry on. My father could never have known amidst his reflections that this generation would be the last, that all of his Prussian traditions would disappear forever in just a few short years.

Just before 9:00 p.m. I announced my arrival in the traditional manner. Hearing my cry, Father rushed in (as all fathers do) and learned to his delight that his second-born was a son. He would honor me with his names, Arthur Oscar Naujoks. My 18-month old sister Waltraut Erika was undoubtedly thrilled to have a noisy younger brother with whom to contend. Happy that all of my fingers and toes were accounted for, father hitched Lotte to the sled to return the midwife to her village. As he drove on through the quiet fairyland of glittering snow and icicles, the fluffy clouds opened to a dazzling panorama of stars that sparkled like crystals against the deep blue winter sky. It was, as he later shared with me, one of the happiest moments of his life. How blessed I was to have been born into this family!

* * * * * *

After losing Vilnius to Poland in 1920, Lithuania seized the Memel area of East Prussia in 1923. The annexation was part of a land-grabbing frenzy that flourished under the ambiguous terms of the Versailles Treaty of 1919. The treaty attempted to provide a legal framework for independence and sovereignty. Though annexation was officially frowned on, it was nonetheless sanctioned under the rationale that such actions could readily be appealed by Germany through the good, though ineffective, offices of the League of Nations.

Solidifying its claim to the Memel area, Lithuania announced to the Germans, who constituted 90% of the population living there, that by May 1924, those who remained in the area would become Lithuanian citizens.[1] Germans who wished to leave the Memel area could take only their clothing, furniture and personal items. All farm implements, tools, and livestock would remain behind with the farms, which would be forfeit to the Lithuanians. For my parents, the choice was easy. They were Prussian Germans and had no desire to become Lithuanians. In the spring of 1924, they packed their belongings into a wagon, borrowed a horse, and headed southwest across the Memel River, back into East Prussia. Barely 15 months old, I sat on my grandma's lap in the front of the wagon as we left our farm and its beautiful meadows behind. My infancy blessed me with no memory of the sorrow and loss my parents felt as they drove away from their home. As events came to pass, I never returned to my birthplace.

My father found work near Tilsit, which provided our family with a home. Germany was in the depths of postwar depression and inflation was at its worst; the poor economy fell hard on the people of East Prussia. With German currency turning worthless overnight, bartering became the economy of survival. It was useless to trade in currency where 10 million marks was required to mail a letter.[2]

In a barter economy, it was a blessing to live in a rural area where food could still be produced in abundance and families could survive. Food was plentiful. We had milk, butter, eggs, vegetables, poultry, beef, pork and fish. Mother's meals were hardy and filling and provided more nourishment than a young boy could burn on an active day in the country. Our stomachs were tempered into cast iron by Mother's coarse dark rye breads and rich cooking.

My father worked on one of the large farms outside Tilsit, known as a *Gutshof.* The farm had about 30 horses and other livestock. It was my father's job to care for these animals and keep them in top working condition. He spent many long nights in the stable helping with a newborn foal or calf, or doctoring a sick animal. Father also served as coachman for the landowners. Often, when he needed to drive people into town or go for supplies or errands, he would swing me up into the seat beside him for a day of adventure and good company. For hunts, he was the head teamster of the wagons that would carry food and equipment for the gentry as they chased fox or hunted stag and moose in the Prussian forests.

Besides his livery responsibilities, my father also worked long hours in the fields. Because we had arrived with almost nothing, Father had no choice but to do everything asked of him. In return, we had a home, plenty of food, and relative security. However, it came at a stiff price: long hours, sweat and tears; but this still could not break my father's spirit or his resolve to provide the best for his family. All of us pitched in to help where we could. Wages were small and money was scarce, but we were able to supplement our income by raising pigs, chickens, geese and ducks. Such goods were always in high demand in Tilsit.

Our home at the *Gutshof* was fairly modern. It had three rooms and a loft, and a cellar for storage. Indoor plumbing and electricity brought us firmly into the 20th century with a standard of living that was not enjoyed by all in East Prussia. Though the house was drafty in the winter, Mother kept us warm with a cozy fire, hot meals and plenty of blankets at bedtime. In the summer, a cool breeze would blow through the house in the evenings, making midsummer nights pleasant and comfortable. It was a small home, but we were content and we were happy.

* * * * * * *

As a child growing up on a farm in East Prussia, my horizons were limited only by my imagination, and my boundaries defined only by my endurance. Life was full, and there was never a want for something to do. I had many friends, and we ranged far and wide across the countryside surrounding the *Gutshof* in search of adventure. Even work with my father was exciting. We exercised the horses across the fields and meadows and hunted rodents in the barn and in the fields.

Sometimes I rode with my father on the tractor as he hauled hay or plowed the fields.

A railroad ran nearby – the line between Ragnit and Tilsit. My friends and I found a small, corrugated metal maintenance shed next to the track with a stove inside. We claimed squatters' rights, and it became our clubhouse. Many times trains would rumble by within a handshake of our hideout. What a sight we must have been to passing engineers - bright-eyed and bushy-tailed, peering out of the grimy window as smoke curled out of the stovepipe.

Some of the pastimes of children in East Prussia were not unlike those of American children, such as the never-ending adventures of cowboys and Indians. Karl May had introduced such escapades to German children through the stories of Chief Winnetou and Old Shatterhand.[3] Stoically, we had taken up the responsibility of clearing East Prussia of outlaws and Indians. A friend's father, who was a machinist, fashioned our firearms out of old pipe and scrap metal. Headdresses with colorful feathers, tomahawks and spears were also carefully crafted for battle. Our most treasured weapons for this crusade, however, were the bows made from hardwoods complete with arrows made from the straight branches of plum trees. Though hardly lethal, they looked real.

When we tired of cowboys and Indians, we headed for the forest where lakes and rivers provided all sorts of adventure. We spent many a summer night camping by a lake in crude pup tents and blankets, a far cry from the relative luxury that backpackers enjoy today. Ghost stories around the campfire, practical jokes and short-sheets ensured that no one ever got any sleep. And when everyone finally settled down, just lying on your back staring into the billions of stars sprayed across the heavens made sleep the last thing on anyone's mind. God was so close; all you had to do was lie there, listen, and learn the secrets of eternity.

* * * * * *

East Prussia was a part of the world that was very ancient in many ways. The southeast shore of the Baltic Sea was already settled by the first millennium B.C. It was the meeting point for three major cultures: the Finno-Ugric, Germanic and Slavic.[4] This confluence resulted in many traditions and myths that continue to influence the region to this day.

Generally speaking, the pagan religions, which existed before the Teutonic Knights brought Christianity to Prussia, worshiped things in nature. They believed the animals of the forest, especially the wolf, were sacred manifestations of pagan deities. Indeed, the trees themselves received offerings for the sacred spirits that dwelled within them. Central to this blend of Indo-European cultures was the importance of the sun, moon and stars, and a symbolic veneration of fire. The worship of the sun and its cycles was a common recurring theme throughout much of Europe during this period, manifested in a variety of festivals that were remarkably similar – from the plains of Stonehenge, to the seven hills of Rome, to the forests of the Baltic.[5]

When Christianity came to the region of the Baltic, it took on characteristics of religious dualism, combining pagan traditions and mysteries with Christian symbols and rhetoric. The pagan festivals continued, only under Christian names.[6] Natalis Solis, or birth of the sun, was celebrated by the Romans on December 25 of the Julian calendar adopted by Julius Caesar in 46 B.C. This celebration of the beginning of the ascension of the stars and sun, which we now associate with the winter solstice, easily became a celebration of the nativity we now celebrate as Christmas. Even to this day, we venture to the forest at Christmastime to fetch a tree to adorn with our offerings and gifts.

Christmas in East Prussia was a special time. On Christmas Eve all the church bells in the cities and villages would ring for about twenty minutes, which filled you with a sense of peace and holiday spirit. As the evening progressed, families would gather at the churches for evening services, carols and fellowship among friends and neighbors. After church, we would return to our homes, light the Christmas tree, and exchange gifts with family and loved ones. With a Yule log blazing in the fireplace and plenty of Christmas treats, Christmas Eve was the high point of the season. We usually had Christmas Day and the following day as holidays, which were often needed to recover from the excitement of Christmas Eve.

At the opposite end of the solar cycle was the summer solstice, the midsummer night made famous by Shakespeare. It is the midpoint between the vernal and autumnal equinox, where the geographical position of the sun reaches its highest latitude over the Tropic of

Capricorn; the shortest night of the year. The Christian name given to this festival in honor of John the Baptist was St. John's Eve, or Johanninacht, as we called it in East Prussia.

Tradition dies hard in Germanic and Slavic lore, and so it was with Johanninacht. Each year on June 23rd we would prepare a barrel full of wood and pitch. When the long summer day would finally end in the late evening, the barrel would be lit and hoisted up a pole twenty-five to thirty feet in the air, usually on top of a hill. The barrel would burn long into the night as family and friends gathered below to enjoy the spectacle of other torches burning across the countryside. Children would sit still as older folks sang traditional songs, played the harmonica and told stories passed down from generation to generation. Legends of the forest, stories of ancestors and accounts of their own lives all played before us as we watched the stars wiggle in the invisible heat waves that rolled up from the burning barrels. It was on such a night that I learned of my Salzburger ancestors and their journey to Prussia. I listened to stories about my grandfathers in the Prussian Cuirassiers, and about my father's capture on the Western Front on that very same day, only a few years before. It was a magical night, and no matter how many times you heard a story, Johanninacht was the time to hear it again. On that night they became indelibly etched into one's memory; the stories I heard on Johanninacht are the ones I remember to this day.

* * * * * * *

One week after Easter in 1928 I attended my first day of school. I was very excited! My mother had to go with me the first day to see that I was properly registered and oriented to my new surroundings. In the summertime, the 45-minute walk to school was easy and fun, especially among the many classmates with whom I walked. In the winter, however, the trip could be long and tiring.

In Germany, children attended public school from age six to fourteen. Wealthy children often started earlier in Kindergarten and entered gymnasium before their fourteenth birthday. Gymnasiums were private schools where most graduates became professionals such as lawyers, doctors, scientists and the like. Only the wealthy could afford to send their children to gymnasium, a school that I couldn't even dream of attending.

At age six, I entered *Die Siebende Klasse*, or 7th grade. In Germany, we began at 7th grade and graduated from the 1st grade. Our school had separate classrooms for each grade, as well as separate wings for boys and girls. Our teachers were strict and enforced discipline with a long stick kept behind the desk. Talking back to a teacher was unheard of in my school; we craved the opportunity to learn and let nothing get in the way of our education. My father had taught me from my earliest days that knowledge was power, that my education was the ticket that would open new horizons of opportunity that had been unavailable to him. I was determined to use the skills of hard work and discipline that he had given me to get the best education possible.

We learned by memorization our entire math tables, rules of language, historical dates, names and places, and famous quotations. We learned to write with ink and pen, and express ourselves concisely and articulately. We studied the great poets, philosophers, musicians and writers; most of those we came to know were German!

Each class had its own *Schule-Mütze*, or school cap, made from nice material with a distinctive ribbon to identify each class. When Hitler came to power, however, these caps were banned. Each class was known by its Latin name, such *as classis septimus* and consisted of about 25 boys (or girls, depending on which wing of the school you attended!). During the first year, school began at 9:00 a.m. and ended before lunch. Older children attended from 8:00 a.m. and were always finished by 1:00 p.m. During the summer months, the school would sponsor track and field events in the afternoons at facilities next to the school. In the winter, we would move indoors for gymnastics and other indoor sports during the same time period.

Germany placed a high premium on the education of its youth, and the facilities we had in our public schools were top-notch. Our classrooms were well equipped, our books were current, and our sports facilities were impressive. Though the Weimar Republic was ineffective and our economy was in shambles, the education system, at least in East Prussia, survived intact through the disastrous depression years of the twenties.

In 1930 I moved to a new school near Tilsit, the *Neustadtische-
Volkeschule*, which was larger and had more students. I began fifth grade
at this school and eventually graduated in 1937 in my fourteenth year.

* * * * * * *

The move to a new school was the result of a much larger chain of
events that marked a major turning point for our family. Almost without
warning, the large *Gutshof* where we had lived for almost six years was
sold and parceled into smaller farms. My father wanted to buy one of
the parcels and continue farming. He had the parcel all picked out, but
my mother had had enough. She was through with farming and all the
hard work, long hours and tears that were necessary to survive as a
farmer. It was time to move to the city, and this development presented
the opportunity to make a new beginning.

My father had also received an offer of employment in Tilsit about
this same time to work at one of the town's two main breweries. So he
hung up his farm boots and headed back to school to become a
brewmeister. For Father, it was a new and exciting career; for the rest
of us, it was an opportunity to enjoy the conveniences of the city and
the profitable fruits of Father's labors.

We moved into a large, four-unit building that might best be
described as a townhouse in modern real estate terms. It was a new
home with a huge yard in which to play. Though we had lived in many
different places, our home was always a haven. It became the anchor

that secured us through the stormy decade of the thirties. Though a Russian bomb would eventually destroy our last house in Tilsit on April 20, 1943, I still remember it as the castle that sheltered and protected us from events that were overtaking Germany and East Prussia. It was there that we prepared to face the horrors of war and, against incalculable odds, eventually survive intact as a family.

* * * * * * *

In 1937, at the age of fourteen, I graduated from the public schools, eager to continue my education. My grades and test scores were excellent and warranted my going on to college. Our family, however, did not have the financial resources to send me. Nevertheless, I had it in my mind that I wanted to attend *Die Industrie und Handel-Schüle* (College for Industry and Commerce), and I convinced my parents that I could work to earn my tuition. I knew that if I could complete the two-year curriculum, I would stand an excellent chance to get a higher paying job and take advantage of even greater opportunities this would present. My family agreed, and by rearranging priorities and sacrificing here and there, I was able to enter the college with the next class.

Our curriculum consisted of advanced general topics, such as geography, foreign languages, math and typing, and specialized classes related to business management—banking, shorthand, bookkeeping and other related subjects. I enjoyed my classes immensely and felt that, finally, I had the break I needed to change my standing in society.

On the main street in our city, there was a popular delicatessen where I decided I would like to work while going to school. One afternoon I visited the owner, and by the next morning I was sweeping the floor and stocking the shelves. It was a good, honorable job, worthy of a business student.

One afternoon the grocer called me in and handed me some papers. He told me that I was to pick up some goods from the railroad station. As I turned to leave, he told me I would find a handcart in the back of the store, which I would need to haul the shipment back to the store. The cart was large, with two wheels as tall as myself. With some degree of effort I pushed it to the railroad depot, retrieved the goods, and struggled back to the delicatessen. As I unloaded the cart, I realized that I was still a manual laborer, no different from the other workers at the depot who had no education at all. Though my observations may have been those of a young, immature teenager, I was nevertheless filled with the resolve I needed to complete my college education. I would never again allow myself to be confined to the ranks of common laborers with dreams and ambitions that could never be fulfilled for lack of an education.

Growing up in Tilsit provided a wide spectrum of experiences for me. I faced challenges, some of which I easily overcame. Others could never be conquered for the simple reason that the lines of Prussian society were drawn along sharp social creases. East Prussians drew lines between the rich and the poor, the landed and the tenant, and the political majority and the oppressed minority. East Prussians looked down on those religious beliefs that were not accepted, as opposed to those that were taken for granted. I found myself on the outside the acceptable majority. Looking back, I am grateful for the social obstacles I chose to overcome. I am proud that, in some instances, I refused to compromise my political and religious beliefs to become socially acceptable, especially with regard to my religious beliefs.

CHAPTER 3

COME THE SAINTS

ONE AFTERNOON IN 1928, while we still lived at the *Gutshof*, my mother heard a knock at the door. She opened it to find two well-dressed young men struggling to communicate with her in something that sounded like German, but for the most part was unintelligible. After some degree of effort, she learned that they were missionaries from America. Surprised and impressed by their politeness, she invited them in. During the next hour or so, she and my grandmother were able to determine that these young missionaries were from Utah and were members of The Church of Jesus Christ of Latter-day Saints. Neither my mother nor grandmother had ever heard of Mormons before, and thus had no preconceived prejudices or dispositions toward their beliefs. Indeed, our family's Salzburger legacy of religious tolerance provided our family with open and inquisitive minds, receptive to these new discussions.

As the afternoon passed, Mother invited them to stay for dinner. They continued to talk about their homeland and experiences while Mother prepared the meal. Father arrived from the fields and was astounded to find Americans sitting in his house. Far from being offended, he marveled that not too many years before, Germans stood in trenches pointing their rifles at Americans who were considered the enemy. He was proud to welcome these young men to his home and grateful there was no ill will remaining between Germans and

Americans. He, too, enjoyed their stories and descriptions of a place he had never heard of, a place that seemed almost too good to be true.

As the Elders sat up to the table, my mother became concerned that they may not be ready for her hardy menu. Somewhere she had developed the belief that Americans preferred a bland diet of refined foods. But, as she watched them pack dinner away, she decided that cast iron stomachs must have been installed before these missionaries had been sent to East Prussia.

For the next several weeks, my family was taught the doctrines of the Latter-day Saints. We learned we could live together forever, and that there were significant differences between Protestant-Catholic Christianity and the ancient Christian beliefs, which had been reestablished in the "Mormon" Church by Joseph Smith in 1830. My parents read *Das Buch Mormon*, which was believed to be the account of an entire civilization on the American continents that had been visited by Christ and taught the same principles we knew from the New Testament.

My mother and grandmother were the first to be baptized, on June 7, 1928. Then, as my sisters and I reached the age of eight, we too were baptized. My baptism took place in the late spring of 1931, a few months after my eighth birthday. I was baptized in the Memel River on a summer evening, not far from where Napoleon and Czar Alexander had met on a barge to decide the fate of Prussia over a century before. It was also only a year after the centennial anniversary of the founding of the Church by Joseph Smith. My father was baptized not long after me, on September 13, 1931, in the same Memel River.

Several Prussians in the Tilsit area were Mormons, and a branch had been established there for some time. The Tilsit branch quickly became the center around which our lives revolved. Our closest family friends came to be the members of our branch in Tilsit. Our social and recreational calendar mirrored the activities of the branch. Of course, Sundays were always filled with meetings and responsibilities. Our family had grown to five. In addition to Waltraut and me, little Elly came along in 1930, making our family complete.

Over the years we entertained many missionaries in our home. They seemed to be the closest link we had to the headquarters of the Church in far-off Salt Lake City, and we loved to hear them describe home, and tell us about the pioneers and real Indians!

Our branch consisted of roughly 110 members on paper, but only 60 to 75 were ever active at one time. We met in a rented space that was a former billiard and beer hall. The lingering smell of old tobacco smoke was unpleasant, sometimes making it almost impossible to breathe. On Sundays, we divided the large hall into classrooms by hanging curtains on cords spanning the hall. Our surroundings were humble and sometimes unpleasant, yet we always looked forward to our meetings and activity nights. Without question, the social event of the year was a gala New Year's Eve party held at the meetinghouse, complete with refreshments and a stunning array of cakes and sweets.

When I became a Deacon, my closest circle of friends was within the Aaronic Priesthood of our branch. We did everything together. In good weather, we would spend the afternoon after Sunday school bicycling or hiking through the countryside. We were all members of the Pathfinders, a Church program similar to American Boy Scouts, and we spent time camping and hiking together. We proudly wore our uniforms of green shirts and brown shorts with a neckerchief and a brown pine tree emblem.

In winter, as Aaronic Priesthood holders, we had the responsibility of arriving at the meeting hall early to build a fire in the tile-lined oven. The heat from the fire vented through the heating flues and up the chimney, heating other tiles that eventually warmed the building. After each meeting where the Sacrament was administered, we washed and polished the glass Sacrament cups and then carefully put them away. Deacons did not have to collect fast offerings because members included such offerings with their tithes.

Being a Saint in East Prussia during the 1930s was not easy. Everyone in town knew our meeting hall as the place where the crazy Mormons met. They knew nothing about our beliefs, thinking falsely that Mormons still had many wives. The missionaries who came to East Prussia over the years worked hard. However, they encountered few willing to give up their Protestant or Catholic traditions or even take time to hear the missionaries' message.

Our branch was our extended family. My Aaronic Priesthood brothers were just that – brothers; brothers in the closest sense of the word. Though we were thousands of miles from Church headquarters, the Church provided the same organization in East Prussia as existed in Utah. We may not have had the long- standing family pioneer traditions that Utah wards enjoyed, but we had the same Young Men's and Young Women's Mutual Improvement Associations; we had the same Relief Society and Priesthood organizations; and, most important, we had the same principles of the gospel. What we knew as *Die Glaubens Artikel,* Americans knew as the *Articles of Faith.* When Americans sang *We Thank Thee, O God, for a Prophet,* we sang *Wir Danken Dir Herr fur Propheten.* In either language, the meaning was the same.

Yet while these similarities did exist, what was different in the 1930s was the contrast between the secure environment that American Mormons enjoyed, and the uncertainty and fear that existed for German Mormons. In this light, few Americans of my generation have ever been able to understand how important the Church - its programs and its priesthood - were to the well-being of German Saints.

When I was ordained a Deacon, Adolf Hitler had been in power for two years. By 1935, *Die Deutsches Jungvolk* (The German Young Folk for boys age 10 to 14) and *Die Hitlerjugend* (The Hitler Youth for boys age 15 to 18) were fast becoming the official organizations for young men in Germany. Outwardly, the Hitler Youth embraced ideals of physical fitness, a love of the outdoors and loyalty to the Thousand-Year Reich. However, noticeably absent from the Hitler Youth program was a love for God or family. Indeed, the Nazis sought to downplay all identity with self, or with a family unit, and to replace it with a loyalty for the *Deutscher Volk*.

It seemed the NSDAP,[1] or Nazis as we remember them, wanted to replace our loyalty to family and country with a religious worship of Hitler as the singular symbol of the German nation. For many Saints in Germany, it appeared the Nazis were trying to create a profanely distorted imitation of our Church organization. What was obviously wrong with the Nazi approach was illustrative of what was wrong with much of the world - the absence of God, elimination of individual identity, and debasement of the family unit.

Many Saints watched helplessly as the German people were hypnotically seduced by the charismatic patriotism of Hitler. Yet in retrospect it is easy to see how the German people were quick to embrace the colorful regalia, the overblown pomp and ceremony, and the alluring, mysterious rituals of the Nazis. The Germans were desperate people who had endured almost 15 years of humiliation and economic destitution with no meaningful leadership. Hitler offered an easy means of resolving the past by simply placing the blame for all of Germany's woes onto others.

Before Hitler came to power, most Germans believed the greatest threat to our security came from the political left. With high unemployment, uncontrollable inflation, and political disunity, Communism was fast becoming the most popular political position.

Also, looming just to the east was the ever-threatening presence of Stalin and his evil Soviet Empire. The NSDAP came from the radical right, the political polar opposite of communism. Thus, capitalist Germans saw Hitler as the answer to the growing communist threat.

When Hitler put people back to work, built the *autobahns* and rearmed the military, his fanatical totalitarian style and controlled economy were an acceptable inconvenience to insure safety from the communists. Hitler's economic success made him ever more popular among Germans who had endured the terrible hardships of the depression of the 1920s.

From my perspective as a member of the Aaronic Priesthood in the 1930s, the shadow of Hitler was always there, but it never prevented me from being an active member of the church. We were never forbidden to meet, and we were never harassed by brownshirts. We were like most other German citizens as our lives gradually became controlled by a totalitarian police state. We were concerned about our right to meet as a branch and continue our church activities, so resistance was not considered advisable.

We watched the injustice that was heaped upon the Jews of Tilsit. The yellow stars appeared, and signs went up warning us not to buy goods from Jewish-owned businesses. Though we despised the obvious persecution, we were also sensitive to the fact that such treatment could be turned on us as well.[2] Yet even knowing that our Jewish neighbors were being harassed, beaten and abused, no one was capable of believing what was truly happening. Even with the knowledge we have today, the horrors of the Holocaust are still difficult to understand.

In the Tilsit Branch, we continued our meetings uninterrupted. We continued to preach and study the gospel, entertain investigators, support the missionaries and build the kingdom however we could. None of our Aaronic Priesthood group joined the Hitler Youth, preferring instead to continue with our Pathfinder program. On December 1, 1936, just before I became a Teacher, Baldur von Schirach succeeded in having a law passed that declared:

> The entire German youth within the borders of the Reich is organized in the Hitler Youth. . . It is not only in home and school, but in the Hitler youth as well that all of Germany's youth is to be educated, physically, mentally, and morally, in the spirit of National Socialism to serve the nation and the racial community.[3]

Though the law made membership in the Hitler Youth compulsory, we continued as Pathfinders and ignored the brownshirts. During this period I was in the last years of my public schooling, in which I attended class from Monday through Saturday. Membership in the Hitler Youth, however, allowed you to take Saturdays off, so the entire weekend could be spent marching in the woods, taking part in athletic games and other Nazi activities. As more and more of my classmates joined the program, our class size dwindled. Soon it seemed the only students in school were Mormons.

On March 25, 1939, a new law was passed that made membership mandatory.[4] All German youth had to be registered by their parents or guardians, who risked fines and imprisonment if they did not comply. Schoolteachers informed those who did not attend Hitler Youth that school would no longer be held on Saturdays and that everyone should join the Hitler Youth immediately, which many of us reluctantly did. I told my mother I did not want a brown shirt though, and because I was never in uniform, I was always put at the end of the line. Our branch president told us the Pathfinders had been outlawed, and we were no longer allowed to have any Pathfinder activities. Still, my friends and I ducked out of Hitler Youth activities and carried on by ourselves, not as Pathfinders or Hitler Youth, but as friends who shared the same religious beliefs.

No one discussed politics. We wanted to avoid problems that could possibly arise from comments or statements that could in any way be considered critical of the Nazis. Even more sobering was the possibility that someone in the branch might be associated with the Gestapo or SS. We did not need to be told that circumspection and silence were appropriate; we just knew. It was important for all the members of our branch family that the Mormons were viewed as loyal, law-abiding Germans, though it was hard for some and required the true exercise of faith. The Twelfth Article of Faith was clear: we were subject to the law of our homeland.

Our branch president was Otto Schulzke, a short man who was always stern. He was a *Beamter*, or civil servant, who eventually emigrated to Utah after the War. His son Heinz was one of my good friends with whom I spent time kayaking on the Memel (Nieman) River. Heinz and I were eventually drafted into the army on the same day and walked to the train station together to go to war. He went to Königsburg and was assigned to a communications center at a headquarters near Berlin. He was mechanically inclined, able to repair typewriters blindfolded. After the War he moved to Utah with his family, working for years for Schnieyer Typewriters in Salt Lake City.

My best friend was Kurt Bratz. His father was about the same age as my father, and our families were close. It was to their home outside Tilsit that Kurt and I usually rode our bicycles on Sunday afternoon.

Kurt was younger than I and very intelligent. He was drafted into the army after me and was assigned as a Panzer Grenadier in a light armor unit. In 1943 he was severely wounded on the Eastern Front, losing his eyesight, an arm and a leg. He died shortly after returning to Tilsit.

Kurt's cousin Siegfried Meischuss was also a close member of our circle of friends. He was quiet, but always a true and loyal comrade. Siegfried trained for three years as an apprentice in prosthetics. Unfortunately, he was eventually drafted and died in 1944 from wounds he received when his armored personnel carrier was hit by artillery in Yugoslavia. His sister Helga eventually married and moved to Salt Lake City, naming her son after her brother. Her son Siegfried Meyer established a popular delicatessen in Salt Lake City known simply as *Siegfried's*.

Another of our group of friends was Berthold Flach, who was the youngest. Berthold's parents were divorced. I never met his father, who had moved away to Africa. His mother was financially secure, however, having come from a well-to-do family. Berthold's sister, Anna Marie, was my girlfriend, so naturally I spent a lot of time visiting the Flach home. Anna Marie went to acting school but never became an actress.

Like Heinz Schulzke, Berthold was also mechanically inclined and liked to fix things. Very patient and friendly, he had a strong testimony and loved being a member of our Aaronic Priesthood group. Berthold was killed instantly when the panzer tank he was driving on the Eastern Front suffered a direct hit.

To some, these dead comrades are nothing more than faceless Nazi soldiers who deserved to die because the cause of the Third Reich was immoral and evil. To me, they were my friends. We shared a common belief in our religious principles and a love for our church and its members. As Christians, we hated war; but as Prussians, we knew it was our duty to fight for our homeland, just as our fathers and grandfathers had done before us. It was the law of our land, and a conscientious objection was something we were not even remotely prepared to consider.

Other members of the Church in Germany during this same period
heroically risked and sometimes lost their lives challenging the immoral
conduct of the Nazis.[5] They exercised their free agency and decided to
take a different path than I. In hindsight, we know them to be heroes
with incredible fortitude. Still, the decisions they made were no more
difficult than the decisions others made to exercise faith, to obey the law
of the land, and to take up arms against other human beings.

I look back at the events of my life during those years and know
that the beliefs and principles I embraced as a member of my church
became a rod that guided me through the war. As soldiers, most
decisions that affected our lives were made by others. As Saints,
however, we made our own choice to follow God's laws as expounded
in Section 58 of the *Doctrine and Covenants* of our church. Whatever the
consequences, we knew that obedience to these instructions, even at the
cost of our lives, was the only way we could find our way through the
otherwise insane and evil world of war.

Many of my friends died in that faith. Yet their faith lit the same fire
that burned within me; a testimony that saw me through unbelievable
horror. And though I have survived in this life, I know that they have
survived to an even greater life. I know they have a perfect knowledge
of what their sacrifice meant. It was not a sacrifice for the Fatherland,
but a sacrifice for their faith and beliefs and obedience to a higher law
that transcends the feeble efforts of man to make sense out of what is
senseless.

CHAPTER 4

STORM CLOUDS

As A COLLEGE student, I learned about new materials known in German as *Ersatz*, meaning substitute or synthetic materials. For several years, German science had been focusing on changing or compounding different molecules to produce new materials, such as a synthetic rubber known as *Buna* made from isobutylene and other ingredients. While most of the world travels today on synthetic rubber, in the 1930s its development was one of the primary strategic goals of German industrialists.

In the late 1920s a secret agreement was struck between the giant German industrial corporation, I.G. Farben, and Standard Oil of New Jersey. They agreed to recognize their respective monopolies in the chemical and petroleum industries. Standard Oil of New Jersey agreed to recognize and honor I.G. Farben patent rights in the chemical industry, including synthetic rubber, in return for Standard Oil of New Jersey's exclusive control over the petroleum industry. The net effect was a line drawn in the sand between the two industrial giants that neither would cross. When war finally came to America over a decade later, Missouri's Senator Harry Truman would discover this international corporate pact and regard it as nothing less than treason. The failure of America to develop synthetic rubber production infuriated the future American president.[1]

As the world mobilized, the demand for gasoline and motor oil increased dramatically. Owing to the American control of the oil industry, German scientists worked feverishly to find a chemical substitute. In coal they found an answer. German scientists developed two methods to convert this fossil fuel into fuel oil, one known as *Bergius-hydrogenation*, and the other known as the *Fischer-Tropsch method*.[2]

Hydrogenation is a process where hydrogen is combined with unsaturated organic compounds to yield a great variety of synthetic products used both in the laboratory and in industry. A good example of a product made through hydrogenation is margarine. Large volumes of cheap and plentiful vegetable oils that are normally unpleasant in taste and odor are combined with hydrogen at temperatures of almost 400 degrees Fahrenheit to produce a tasteless and odorless lard-like substance. This substance is then turned into margarine and cooking oils. Other products made through hydrogenation and unsaturated organic compounds include soap and wax.

A German scientist named Frederich Bergius developed a process whereby coal and coal tar is mixed with heavy oil and ground into a fine paste. The paste and oil are then hydrogenated under pressure through three processes, resulting in gasoline. One ton of coal could yield about 80 gallons of gasoline.

Franz Fischer and Hans Tropsch developed the more popular method used by the Germans in the 1930s. The Fischer-Tropsch method used a mixture of carbon monoxide and hydrogen gases with a catalyst containing nickel, cobalt or modified iron to produce synthetic petroleum and diesel fuels. Many of today's popular synthetic motor oils are made through this or very similar processes. This method is also used widely today in producing synthetic fats and soaps.

By 1939, German hydrogenation plants were producing two million metric tons of synthetic fuels; by 1943, this production would increase to over 4.6 million metric tons per annum.[3] It was the fuel that drove the Wehrmacht. The two-dozen plants that were built throughout Germany to produce synthetic fuels were primary targets of British and American bombers. Beginning in 1944 through April 1945, British and American bombers dropped 123,584 tons of bombs on these plants, bringing Germany's synthetic fuel production to a virtual halt, along with the wheels of the Wehrmacht.[4]

* * * * * * *

I graduated from college in early 1939 and bid farewell to my friends and classmates. Our idyllic days as students were over. The real world was upon us as we each set out to complete a 30-month internship required of all students after graduation. We had to find our own employment and then complete the internship with our employer. Following the internship, we would all undergo an examination before a board of the Chamber of Commerce.

I quickly found employment with an industrial company called *Horstigall*, which specialized in agricultural manufacturing and construction. We built products mostly from wood, ranging from beer barrels to large industrial silos. Although the work was interesting and challenging, it was not my first choice. It lacked the glamour of the more sophisticated synthetics industry in which I had a keen interest.

Once again, I started at the bottom. However, my employer was mindful of my need to qualify by examination and gave me the opportunity to become completely acquainted with all of the departments in the company. After my two-and-a-half-year apprenticeship, I was well prepared for my examination and passed with flying colors.

In the interim, the face of Germany was changing rapidly. I could no longer regard the Nazis with the devil-may-care attitude that routinely led my friends and me to ditch Hitler Youth activities in favor of our own. The totalitarian domination the Nazis exercised over all aspects of our lives was a force to be reckoned with. For years we had hailed the economic turnaround and the advances in technology and industry that had been made by Hitler. The price we had paid for this turnaround, however, was an increasing sacrifice of personal freedom - the freedom to think and act as our conscience dictated. Perhaps it is easy to say in hindsight that we did not see this coming or that Germany was deceived. But in reality, Germany walked into National Socialism with its eyes wide open. We modified our lifestyle; when the Nazis created a pinch, we made adjustments. We avoided trouble and found ways to work within the system.

For some, however, this tacit acceptance was impossible. My Uncle Max Loeper was one of those who could not bend with the winds of Nazi change. During my years of college and apprenticeship I watched my grandmother fret over her eldest son and his continuing criticism of Hitler's regime. An avowed socialist, Uncle Max crossed the Memel River at night into Lithuania. He returned with smuggled anti-Nazi literature, which he then distributed within the area.

In 1935 or 1936, Uncle Max was captured and sent to Stuhm Prison where he remained for several years. His wife Elizabeth was told by the Gestapo she must divorce Uncle Max because he was no longer a German citizen, which she did. When he was released from Stuhm, he came to live with us. One afternoon as I sat at the table with Uncle Max, I asked him why he always wore a hat. He stared into my eyes and slowly removed his hat, revealing his totally shaved head.

Uncle Max was not deterred by his years in prison at hard labor. Almost immediately after his release he resumed his trips across the Memel River. Captured once again, he was sent to Sachsenhausen, this time never to return. In March 1941, two Gestapo agents came to our home and informed my grandmother that Uncle Max was dead. If she was willing to pay 65 marks, they would ship the body back to Tilsit for burial. A substantial sum at the time, my grandmother took it from her pension, but Uncle Max was never returned.

Uncle Max's life was filled with tragedy. His youngest daughter, my cousin Irmgard, was not yet four when she died in June 1934. Just over a year later, in September 1935, his oldest son, cousin Heinz, died at the age of seven. Perhaps Uncle Max had a lot of anger and frustration inside of him; perhaps he was simply an idealist who could not tolerate the Nazis. Whatever the reason, Uncle Max paid for his idealism with his life and my grandmother's broken heart.

* * * * * * *

During the 1930s there were two means of communication through which we received most all of our news – the radio and the newspaper. As can be imagined, both of these media were gradually absorbed and controlled by the Nazis.

When Hitler became Chancellor in 1933, Goebbels' Propaganda Ministry assumed control of radio stations, which had been under the control of the Post Office during the Weimar Republic. All radio stations came under the RRG, or Reich Broadcasting Company. The Nazis needed everyone to listen to the radio so they set about making an inexpensive set called the *Volksempfänger,* or people's receiver, and a miniature receiver, which we called *Goebbels' Schnauze* or Goebbels' Big Mouth. It was through the radio that the Nazis had their biggest impact in stirring the German people to support one cause or another, whatever was most expedient for the party.

The radio played folk songs or stirring music by German composers: nationalistic marches and patriotic songs. Often, the government would have special programs designed for the entire nation to gather around and listen. If, for some unexplained reason, you did not have a radio, or had not found yourself near one in time for the broadcast, no matter. In many villages in Germany, the Nazis erected loudspeakers in the town square, which blared the message so loudly that it was almost impossible not to hear what was going on. Fortunately, there were no such loudspeakers in Tilsit. In the early days of the war we would hear news of stirring victories that almost always were followed by the national anthem, *Deutschland Über Alles*.

After the war had begun, Germans were prohibited from listening to foreign radio broadcasts, yet almost everyone would listen to the BBC. In Hamburg, three young Latter-day Saint men began listening to the BBC broadcasts on a small Rola radio in the summer of 1941. Helmuth Hübener and Karl-Heinz Schnibbe would meet at Helmuth's home as often as possible to hear the German-language evening news programs. They both quickly figured out, as we all did, that the BBC accounts were substantially different from RRG reports. They were incensed that Germans were not being told the truth, at least by the RRG.

On some evenings, when Karl-Heinz was unable to attend the broadcast, Helmuth took shorthand notes, which the young men later discussed. Helmuth was especially angry about the deception being perpetrated by the Nazis and the RRG and decided to start leaving leaflets around. As summer turned to fall, they were joined by Rudi Wobbe in an ambitious truth campaign that covertly disseminated leaflets that had been typed by Helmuth in his grandparents' apartment then left in mailboxes, phone booths and other high-traffic areas.

Helmuth was driven by his belief that the truth must be known, though I don't think he realized how many of us already knew. Nevertheless, while I was in army basic training, Helmuth, Karl-Heinz and Rudi were taking enormous risks to ensure as many Germans as possible knew they were being deceived.

In February 1942, all three were arrested by the Gestapo and ultimately put on trial for high treason before the infamous *Volksgerichtshof* in Berlin. On August 12, 1942, Chief Justice Fikeis and his fellow justices, dressed in the crimson robes of their "Blood Court" sentenced Karl-Heinz and Rudi to prison, and ordered Helmuth to be executed. In a remarkable display of courage and dignity, Helmuth stood defiantly before Justice Fikeis and stated, "All I have done is tell the truth. Now it is my turn . . . but your turn will come!"[6] On October 27, 1942, he was guillotined in Alt-Moabit Prison at the age of 17.

Hamburg is a long way from Tilsit, in more ways than one. Though I never knew these three young men in Germany, I later met Karl-Heinz after we both had come to Salt Lake City. Each of us dealt with the Nazis in a different manner, yet in many respects our pain and suffering were similar. It is impossible to say which of us made the right or wrong decision, or if we even had a decision to make at all. Both of us were products of our environment and reacted to situations as they were presented to us. Had either of us been in the shoes of the other, perhaps our actions and the outcome would have been the same; perhaps not. What is certain, however, is that our generation in Germany was not blessed with many opportunities for success. Those of us who were fortunate enough to survive have much to ponder and much for which to be thankful.

Helmuth Hübener died a traitor of the Reich, but today he is revered as a hero in Germany. In America, he is a footnote to history that is gradually becoming better known, especially within The Church of Jesus Christ of Latter-day Saints.

* * * * * * *

By 1938, Germany was in a position to act concerning the many wrongs of the Versailles Treaty that Hitler had sworn to make right. Early in 1938, Hitler stepped up efforts to bring Austria into the Reich, knowing that the world would do little, if anything, to stop him. In spite of the efforts of Austrian Chancellor Kurt von Schuschnigg to head off the inevitable with a plebiscite scheduled for March 13, 1938, the Nazis effectively scuttled the vote by exacting a postponement two days prior to the plebiscite. Schuschnigg resigned, and Austrian President Miklas reluctantly appointed Hitler's puppet Dr. Artur Seyss-Inquart as Chancellor.[7] Overnight Austria came under the control of the Nazis.

While the world had little to say about the *Anschluss*, Germany's intentions toward Czechoslovakia and the Danzig Corridor brought more pronounced reactions from abroad. These issues dealt with

territory where several German citizens still resided that had been taken
from Germany after World War I. My family was especially sensitive to
these issues because we had lost everything when Memelland was
absorbed by Lithuania. Without any compensation whatsoever, our
farm, our livestock and our farm equipment had all been redistributed
to Lithuanians when we were forced to choose between our homeland
and becoming Lithuanians. It was blatantly wrong.

Regardless of who was to blame for World War I, my family had
been affected directly by the unjust manner in which Germany was
punished, and suffered this humiliation and injustice because Germany
could effectively do nothing. Now, upon hearing that Hitler was
retaking territory where Germans lived, we could do little to hide our
satisfaction. On one hand, we rejected the Nazis for the manner in
which they exercised control over our lives. But on the other hand, we
applauded the decisive manner in which Hitler repudiated the unfair
terms of Versailles.

In September 1938, Germany annexed the *Sudetenland* from
Czechoslovakia after months of saber-rattling and threats of invasion.[8]
The annexation came about after Prime Minister Neville Chamberlain
had negotiated through most of September to avoid Hitler's threatened
military action against Czechoslovakia. In the end, Hitler agreed to
occupy the German *Sudetenland* frontiers that had been taken from
Germany after World War I. More than three million Germans were
returned to their homeland, which for Germans was not territorial

aggression, but again, righting the wrongs perpetrated against Germany in the 1920s.

Chamberlain returned to England bearing "Peace with Honor" and an illusory belief that Hitler would handle any future problems through diplomacy. In retrospect, it is hard to imagine that Germany could have been prevented from taking back the *Sudetenland*. England and her allies were no more prepared for war in September 1938 than they were in September 1939 – or September 1940, for that matter. To the extent that Chamberlain prevented armed confrontation over the inevitable and exacted Hitler's promise to negotiate problems in the future, "Peace with Honor" is not too far from the truth. Hitler's future betrayal of that promise would become a major indicator to the world of his true nature.

In March 1939, Hitler completed the total annexation of Bohemia and Moravia, comprising most of what is today the Czech Republic. Of more interest to my family was Germany's retaking of Memelland from Lithuania that same month. Though Prussians welcomed the return of what had been appropriated by the Lithuanians, few of those who had been driven out fifteen years earlier, including my family, had any illusion that reparations would be made for our loss. It was enough that Lithuania was pushed back to its pre-1914 border.

Though these annexations returned much of the land taken from Germany after World War I, the Danzig Corridor, which contained the German states of Posen and West Prussia, with more than three million

German inhabitants, remained a part of Poland. Because of Poland's unique history of dismemberment at the hands of one invader or another, the world was ready to stand fast over Poland. Regardless of German claims to Posen and West Prussia, England and her allies believed Poland's survival as a nation transcended the ethno-nationalist demands of Hitler. The issue continued to fester through the summer of 1939.

* * * * * * *

The spring of 1939 marked the end of my youth. I particularly remember nature waking up from her winter slumber: the storks returning from their winter sojourn in Egypt, the flowers blooming in a million colors, and the song of the nightingale. The only thing unique about the nightingale's song, however, is its lack of originality; its melodious imitations are nevertheless a highlight of an early spring morning in Prussia. The fragrance of blossoms on a cool breeze through an open window will stay with me always. These are the memories of Tilsit that are forever etched in my mind, memories of the last spring of my Prussian homeland that would soon be gone forever.

In the summer of 1939, the word came down that all missionaries must leave Germany. They arranged for passage to Copenhagen, where they boarded a ship to return to America. Suddenly, the Church in Prussia was alone, cut off from Salt Lake City, cut off from the world. At the Mission Home in Berlin, President Klopfer became the effective head of the Church in Germany. He would remain in that position until he was drafted and sent to the Eastern Front, where he eventually died. President Ranglach succeeded him and remained the President of the German Mission until he was released in 1946.

When the news came calling missionaries to Copenhagen, I helped Elder Oscar Sither load his bags onto a handcart, and then hauled them to the train station. I had acquired valuable experience in this skill and was finally putting it to worthy use! I was sad to see the Elders go, but felt relieved that they would get out safely before any serious trouble began.

The serious trouble began early on the morning of September 1, 1939, as German troops crossed the border along a wide front into a defenseless Poland. The news spread through Tilsit like lightning, and immediately all adult males were ordered to assemble at the football stadium. All of us went to the stadium with Father, where he stripped to his underwear. I will never forget the excitement, confusion and fear that filled the stadium that day. Before us we watched Father become a soldier again as he donned a new army uniform, put on his steel helmet, and marched off to the train with his rifle and backpack. The war, which would change my life forever, had begun.

CHAPTER 5

A SOLDIER OF THE REICH

IT WAS SUNDAY morning, June 22, 1941, when my father awoke me at 4:00 a.m. The war was well into its second year, and I had just completed my thirty months of internship. Father had only been gone for three months when they sent him home just before Christmas of 1939, furloughed because of his age. Until now, the war had been uneventful as far as I was concerned. Now, as I brushed the sleep from my eyes, my life was about to change.

All the windows in the house were vibrating. I thought it was a thunderstorm, but as I looked out into the predawn sky, I could see that is was a beautifully clear morning. From the radio we learned that war had begun between Russia and Germany, and Tilsit was part of the front line! The Russians were a mere 20 miles away, and the rumble we could hear was an uninterrupted barrage of artillery fire between the two former allies.

What would happen if our lines were too weak and the German Army had to retreat? What would become of us? We hurriedly packed suitcases and loaded our belongings onto a handcart. Suddenly, at about 6:00 a.m., the air raid sirens began to wail. We were all confused, but I was too excited to be scared. We had no place to go, no place to hide. Moments later, the first bombs began to fall on Tilsit as the Russian bombers droned overhead. But as fast as it began, the air raid was over. In Tilsit, there was property damage but no casualties.

After the air raid, we calmed down a bit and decided that since it was Sunday we ought to go ahead and get ready for Sunday school. After breakfast, I washed up and dressed, but still had time before I had to be at the church. I decided to go down to the quay on the Memel River to see what might be going on.

The thunder of artillery had faded, and from the radio we learned the German Army was advancing on all fronts. At the river I got my first close-up look at the war. Thousands of young Russian soldiers in dirty uniforms, their heads shaved and with frightened looks on their young faces, were being held as prisoners of war. I was amazed that so many Russians had massed on the border near Tilsit. Had Stalin been preparing for war with Germany? I was confused. It would not be until several years after the war that I would learn of the circumstances that led to my first encounter with Operation Barbarossa on that summer solstice of 1941. I stood on the Prussian frontier, gazing once more at an ancient enemy from the east, just as my ancestors had done centuries before.

* * * * * *

Some have said that history is nothing more than the perceptions of those who witness it. To have a complete picture of an event or era is virtually impossible. History becomes the subjective observation of those who recorded the data, took the pictures, and remembered events after the fact. No matter how accurate the data may be from which historians attempt to reconstruct an event, it is always subject to the imperfect influence of human nature. A category of statistics may be omitted; a photograph taken from only one angle, or perhaps even staged; a later memory altered by intervening knowledge learned after the experience took place. All of these variables combine to make history an inexact science, a discipline that is always subject to the influences of newly discovered materials or perspectives.

My brief visit to the quay on the Memel River that morning in 1941 left me with an image that did not fit with the later, politically correct version of history - the unexpected betrayal of and aggression toward Russia by Germany.

Three decades after the end of the war, in 1978, a defecting Soviet official laid documents before British officials describing the buildup of Russian troops along the East Prussian border. The defensive strategy of the Red Army called for reinforcement along the entire border with German-controlled territory. These troops remained poised to strike as early as June 6, 1941. Since the collapse of the Soviet Union, new records have come to light that suggest that Stalin was indeed prepared to launch an attack against Germany. Both Hermann Göring and Alfred Jodl testified before the Nuremberg Tribunal that Germany was aware of the military buildup on its eastern border, and although Barbarossa may have achieved tactical surprise, there was no strategic surprise. The Russians were ready for war.[1] Even though Germany's impending invasion was well known to the Russians through various diplomatic and intelligence channels, Stalin was still indecisive.

The defense plan had been promulgated early in 1941 as the "Special Plan for the Defense of the State Frontier," which essentially was no defense plan at all. The Russians believed the best defense was a good offense. They drafted a plan that called for quick and decisive occupation of German territories supported by an aggressive air campaign.[2] When Russian General Andrei Vlassov was captured in 1942, he told SS Lt. General Richard Hildebrandt the Russian offensive against Germany was scheduled to begin in August or September of 1941. Russian preparations had been slowed by its poor railroad system. When Hitler attacked on June 22, he struck directly into the center of the Russian buildup.[3]

The booming guns on the morning of June 22 caught General F.I. Kuznetsov by "tactical surprise." He desperately began carrying out the defensive plan to take Tilsit and East Prussia as best he could. However, the superior forces of the German Army Group North under the command of Field Marshal Ritter von Leeb soon overwhelmed Kuznetsov's forces. In a matter of hours, thousands of Russian POWs were marching through Tilsit as I headed to my Sunday School class, barely able to hear the artillery moving away into Belorussia.

* * * * * * *

In late August 1941, I was drafted into the German Army. I received my notice about the same time as Heinze Schulzke. We went with our families to the train station early one morning where we also greeted many of our friends, schoolmates and neighbors. As we shook hands and said our farewells, we held on just a little bit longer, wondering if we would ever see one another again. For the most part, none of us ever did.

The train was very long, drawn by two engines already under steam. A band was playing stirring patriotic marches; a huge crowd had gathered to see their Prussian sons off to war once again. Heinz and I crowded into the train. With a shrill whistle the train slowly began to pull out of the station. Tears filled my eyes as I watched my family, my friends, and my youth disappear behind the platform.

As the train rolled out through the countryside, we passed the fields where I had played as a youth. The forests and streams where I had hiked and camped, and even our abandoned hideout on the rail spur all flashed by with increasing speed, a kaleidoscope of my life spinning past the window in a blur. Soon the countryside became unfamiliar; the transition into my new life had begun.

The screech of brakes signaled our arrival at Insterburg, where the first group of draftees got off. The doors opened and German soldiers instructed those leaving the train. I said farewell to Heinz, who continued on to Königsberg, and joined about 200 other young men on the platform. A military band led us through the streets until we arrived at a large, gloomy, gray complex of three-story brick buildings built in the 1920s as a Reserve Training Camp. A *Hauptmann* (Captain) met us and gave us a brief welcoming speech. Afterwards, we organized into groups of 14 men each and were assigned a corporal as our leader. This was the leader who would be responsible for making or breaking us as soldiers; we studied him closely, knowing that in many respects our lives were in his hands.

Our corporal led us into one of the buildings where we found a cold, stark room filled with empty bunks. He assigned each of us a bunk and a locker to hold all of our earthly possessions. Before long we were all looking like recruits ready to begin training.

Our day began at 6:00 a.m. with a loud whistle. We had 30 minutes to shower, shave and dress before breakfast. Our corporal ensured no one slept beyond reveille. At 6:30 we headed for breakfast, and by 8:00 our morning training was underway. Morning classes consisted of training in the use of communications equipment used in artillery spotting. We also learned about the weapons we would be using at the front. Between classes we drilled, learning to walk, march in a goose step and salute. If we made any mistakes, discipline was quick and uncomfortable. After lunch, we usually trained in the classroom learning communications procedures, Morse Code and other skills related to communications between artillery spotters, the battery and regimental headquarters. After 5:00 p.m. the rest of the day was ours to do as we wished. Most of the time we spent preparing for the next day, writing letters home or just relaxing.

After six months of continuous training, we started looking like real soldiers. Our actions and responses were automatic and second nature as we mastered proper communications procedures, the use of weapons, and drill routines of a proper Prussian soldier. We walked the walk and talked the talk as some of the finest trained soldiers of the German Army.

Toward the end of my training cycle, I was appointed to special training known as "OFA" or *Officer Anwärter*. Seventy-five of us separated for special training as junior officers under a strict regimen of advanced leadership and technical training. We learned massive amounts of information dealing with difficult subjects in a limited amount of time. The overwhelming pressure drove almost half of our OFA candidates to quit. Though I thought about it from time to time, I refused to let the pressure get to me. I wanted to succeed in this more than anything else I had ever done.

The 150mm Howitzer particularly interested me. We learned it was capable of shooting a 110-pound artillery round almost 25 miles. It was so big that two teams of six horses were needed to pull the gun carriage and the gun barrel. We learned intricate details from other soldiers who had been at the front and knew everything about handling these guns under combat conditions. We also learned the trigonometric procedures by which these guns could be trained to deliver fire with devastating accuracy.

The firing batteries sat at locations determined with a transit, compass and map. The number two gun was placed as a zero reference point, and guns one, three and four were laid out parallel to the number two gun. Then, with a *Zeil-Spinne* placed at zero over the map, we could get the necessary information for distance and angle on any target. We repeated our firing procedures over and over until we could do it in our sleep. The responsibility delegated to us was enormous; to this day I marvel at the burden each of us bore to insure that these weapons worked correctly.

By the end of OFA training, 45 of us graduated and received one week of well-deserved leave before our unit deployed. Returning to Tilsit, I spent that week in springtime bliss, sleeping in my own bed and eating Mother's cooking (which I had grown to appreciate). I reveled at not having to wake with a whistle or jump when somebody barked a command. I visited friends, neighbors and teachers, describing my adventure of the previous winter. The war was the furthest thing from my mind as I relished every moment of my leave. I even looked up a few of my old girlfriends to ensure that I would not be without mail at the front. The week went by quickly. I enjoyed peace and tranquility, joy and appreciation for my friends and loved ones.

At the end of the week, I repeated my journey by train from Tilsit to Insterburg, knowing that my next move would be to the front. The prospect of future combat combined with leaving my family once again overwhelmed me with a feeling of numbness; I wondered how I could ever carry the responsibilities the army expected of me. The monotonous clack and rock of the train soon had me asleep, still oblivious to any resolution of the fear and excitement that occupied my homesick mind.

Back at Insterburg, everything buzzed with excitement as my OFA graduates rejoined the other recruits and received new battle gear and uniforms. Everything from our boots to steel helmets was new, and it took several days to complete fitting and packing. Finally, we arose one morning and were pronounced fit for duty. We donned our gear and marched with great pride from the camp to the train station through throngs of cheering Prussians. I was proud to be a soldier, proud to be serving my country as my father had, and his father had, back through generation after generation.

From Insterburg we took the train to Königsburg where we joined about 2,000 other newly trained soldiers. After a substantial amount of shouting, cursing, singing and whistling, we managed to crowd onto yet another long train, which we knew was leaving for the front. As the shrill whistle blew again and we began rolling out of the station, one question was on our minds - was it headed to the east or to the west? I struggled all day to watch for any hint of our direction, as the train snaked its way through unfamiliar territory. By evening, I sank back into my seat with an enormous feeling of relief. The farms and villages racing past our window were in Northern Germany. It was obvious that we were still heading west into the setting sun with no hint of turning south or back to the east.

CHAPTER 6

FRANCE

AT THE END of World War I, France determined that two German invasions in less than half a century were enough. After the politically disastrous invasion of the Ruhr Valley by the French in 1923 to "enforce" the reparations terms of the Treaty of Versailles, the French became more preoccupied with their fear of another German invasion from the East.[1] French Minister of Defense, Andre Maginot, launched construction of a sophisticated line of fortifications that stretched from the Swiss border north to the Belgian-Luxembourg border, and south from Switzerland into Southern France. The Maginot Line, as it came to be known, was an impressive defensive array that represented more the obsessive paranoia of French diplomacy than it did state-of-the-art military thinking. Nevertheless, it garrisoned 400,000 highly trained troops, and it set up a formidable obstacle for an invading army.[2]

The German invasion of Poland in September 1939 resulted in war between Germany and the allies, including France. Nonetheless, the lightning strike into Poland caught the western allies by surprise, leaving them at a collective loss about what move to make first. France elected to take a passive stance toward Hitler and did nothing. After the initial panic subsided and no bombs fell in France, a good defense seemed the best offense. Thus began almost nine months of "Sitzkrieg" or the *drôle de guerre* (Phony War). France felt secure in its hopeful assumption the

Maginot Line provided the defense necessary to prevent another bloody war with Germany.[3] In retrospect, perhaps this false sense of security may have indeed saved hundreds of thousands of French lives simply because it forestalled an immediate and prolonged armed confrontation. But then it might also suggest that such a confrontation might have brought Hitler into check and saved millions of other lives.

When France declared war against Germany three days after the blitzkrieg rolled into Poland, hundreds of thousands of French factory workers mobilized to help shoulder the responsibility for defending France, a task that had annihilated the rural peasant farmers in 1914. The immediate result was a slump in the economy and soured public opinion. For the French, there was no winning another war of attrition.

On May 10, 1940, the Phony War came to an abrupt end when General Fedor von Bock and his Army Group B invaded the Netherlands and Belgium, just as the allies had expected. What the allies had not expected was General von Runstadt's Army Group A piercing through the Ardennes, flanking the Maginot Line, and then turning north in a race to the Channel. As allied troops drove into Belgium, unaware of the trap that had been set, General Gerd von Runstadt's 44 divisions blew through the poorly deployed French 2nd and 9th Armies. In less than two weeks, the Germans had crossed the Somme headed for Calais.[4] By May 28, the British were trapped at Dunkirk and the defense of France had all but collapsed. Almost 10 million French civilians fled their homes in one of the largest mass migrations since the

Middle Ages, many of them dying in the withering cross fire between the German and allied armies.

When Paul Reynaud resigned as Prime Minister on June 16, 1940, 84-year-old Marshal Phillipe Petain, a much-beloved hero of World War I, succeeded him. Petain called for France to lay down its arms and end the bloodshed, much to the relief of most of its beleaguered citizens. Less than a week later, Hitler exacted a stiff armistice in the same railroad car that had been the scene of Germany's humiliation in 1918. Petain then set up a puppet government in Vichy, urging the French to work and rebuild an economy that was essential to Germany's strategic needs.[5]

Germany did not prepare for victory in France. As the Germans enjoyed the spoils of victory, the Royal Air Force took the opportunity to regroup. By the time Hitler was ready to invade England, Germany had lost its momentum and was ultimately never able to overcome the fearless defense put up by the RAF during what we now know as the Battle of Britain. By 1942, Operation Sea Lion had been scrapped and France had become a sizable territory for Germany to defend against an invasion that was sure to come.

* * * * * * *

When I arrived in France, it was a beautiful spring morning in April 1942, almost two years after the fall of the Third Republic. Peering out the window as the train began to slow, I saw a sign roll past that read

CALAIS. Calais! I had followed the footsteps of my father, except that this time I was a soldier of the conquering army, not a defeated prisoner of war. Recalling the many wonderful stories of France my father had told my sisters, I expected that my stay in France would be a memorable one.

As our train screeched to a halt at the station in Calais, voices from both ends of the train began yelling *"Alles austeigen!"* ordering us out onto the platform. It was early in the morning, about 7:00 a.m., and all the shouting had been a rude awakening. Still, I was glad to be off the train. As I stretched my weary arms and legs, I watched many French people scurrying about, obviously headed to work early. I couldn't believe I was in France.

As I stood in the morning sun trying to comprehend my situation, the reality of war was suddenly upon us. Nearby the familiar crackle of 20mm antiaircraft flak guns opened up, shattering an otherwise serene morning. Civilians began screaming and running in every direction. I dove for cover and nailed myself to the floor as three RAF Spitfires roared over the station not more than 100 meters above us. They were so close that, had I known the pilots, I would have recognized their faces. For the first time since entering the army, war and the death that accompanies it became a stark reality. The howling Spitfires sent goose bumps from my head to my toes, drilling into me the realization that complete strangers were trying to kill me.

After the Spitfires roared down the track, we dashed out of the station and broke into smaller groups, marching off to some small villages between Calais and St. Omer. None of us wanted to experience any more British hospitality that morning!

Though we were marching south, away from Calais and the Channel, it was still not far enough. London was less than 100 miles away. For the RAF, strafing runs to Calais were an afternoon stroll from their bases around Canterbury and West Maling.

We finally arrived at a small village, the name of which I have long since forgotten but whose charm I can still recall with great fondness. With the ten men assigned to me, I moved into a large farmhouse that had been appropriated by the German Army. Clearly, the French were not pleased with having to quarter German soldiers, but they had no choice in the matter. I immediately sought out the owner of the farm, a woman in her mid-thirties with two children and her parents. She spoke a little German, but I spoke no French! I assured her that we would not harm her or her family in any way, and that, if she had any problems at all, she should come to me directly. Later, as we became better acquainted, she told me her husband was in a prisoner of war camp somewhere in Germany. I began to understand how tragic war can be to a family that at one time led an idyllic life farming in Northern France, only to have their happiness shattered by a war they probably could not understand. Though it was sad, I somehow felt that her husband would likely return intact. It seemed unbelievable to me that Germany was at war with these people. My father had spoken fondly of the French and of Calais. So far his observations had been very accurate, at least from my perspective.

Everywhere we went the French greeted us warmly. The villages and countryside spoke of an old-world charm that remains a fond memory to me half a century later. Yet in the midst of these pleasant surroundings, the shadow of war was never far away.

Many times when I was off duty, I lay in the grass and watched Messerschmidts and Spitfires tangle in the heavens. Puffs of smoke and tracks of machine gun tracers appeared from nowhere signaling a dogfight had commenced. Through my field glasses I watched in wonderment as planes chased each other through the clouds. Finally, one of them silently spiraled below a plume of black smoke, too far away for me to hear the whine of its dying engine. Occasionally, I saw a white puff of a parachute, lowering a lucky pilot to fight another day. But more times than not, a burning aircraft went into its long downward dive to eternity with not so much as a waggle of its wings, its pilot perhaps dead long before it hit the ground.

As many times as I watched this incredible drama of life and death, I could never fully grasp this ritual of war. These men - all of them sons, brothers and even fathers of people who loved them dearly - would climb into an airplane and fly off to kill another son, brother or father flying in another plane – all perfect strangers. But for this deadly meeting in the skies, their lives had likely never crossed paths before and probably would not have crossed in the future. It was all over in a matter of minutes, yet its outcome was permanent and everlasting. At the squeeze of a trigger, a lifetime ended; years of growing up, love and nurturing at the foot of proud and loving parents; hopes and dreams for the future – all of it ended in a charred wreck in the fields of Northern France.

For years I had understood the patriotic responsibility of defending, and even dying for, your homeland. For most Prussians, our loyalty to the Fatherland was almost genetic and never questioned. Yet, as I lay in the grass and watched the tangible result of this loyalty, I suddenly realized that our individual responsibility and purpose in this war went much deeper. It was more than a superficial, almost rhetorical willingness to lay down our lives for the Führer and the Fatherland. The madness of war as a means of resolving political differences seared my mind as I watched this hyperbole of patriotism litter the fields of Northern France with the charred remains of young pilots. They were men not too different from me, having as little or less of a stake in this war as I. Still, every day it went on, like clockwork. After the battle ended and as I lay in the grass lost in my thoughts, returning Messerschmidts glided in low over me, waggling their wings in a victorious sign of a kill. In a few hours, some people in England would receive the news that would change their lives forever. And the next day, I returned to my cheap seats at this Blue Sky Opera House and watched this tragic drama play out again, my mind forever in turmoil.

Dear to the heart of every German were the magnificent words of Friedrich Schiller's *Ode to Joy*. Ludwig von Beethoven put this to music in the fourth movement of his monumental Ninth Symphony, which is today the anthem of a united Europe. As I recalled those lines in the fields of France, I feared Schiller's hope that "all men would become brothers under the protective wings of God" was nothing more than an idealistic hope that might be forever dashed by pride and despotism. War seemed to be the result of a human congenital defect in those few who continued to exercise dominion over common people to effect their political ends.

In France, my new adventure quickly lost its luster. I realized that survival needed to be my primary goal. I knew that, regardless of how I felt about the madness of war, most soldiers who would be attacking me would likely not share the same level of enlightenment. They would be out to kill me, and I expected that I would have to use all of my skill to prevent them from succeeding. Years later, I heard a quote from General Patton that perhaps best summed up my feelings at the time. I learned the object of war was not to die for my country; it was to have the enemy die for his country. It was very base but simple. I was going to have to fight to survive.

* * * * * * *

At the end of April 1942, as I was watching the deadly aerial ballet play out in the skies of France, the Luftwaffe began a series of bombing raids into England on targets in Bath, Canterbury, Norwich, Exeter and York. Hitler was angry over the RAF bombing of civilians in Luebeck and Rostock and decided to order attacks on all buildings in England marked with three stars in the famous Baedeker travel guides. These attacks became known as the Baedeker Raids[6] and resulted in several thousand civilian casualties. At the same time, perhaps expecting a British response, reinforcements moved into Northern France. Our entire Reserve Group became a part of the 376th Infantry Division.

I transferred to the 9th Battery, which operated the powerful 150mm K 18 Howitzers. With our heavy artillery as close to the coastline as possible, we could hit the beaches of Dover from Calais with a hot powder charge. During maneuvers in May, my battery moved to the coastline at Calais where I could see the white chalk cliffs of Dover through the haze with my field glasses. As eager as some of our gunners were to loft a shell to England, I remember our battery commander Hauptmann von Langenstein remarking quietly, "No . . . don't wake up the lion."

Standing in the afternoon sun, I surveyed the vast panorama of the channel before me and the distant cliffs of a country that I only knew from schoolbooks. On our left and right flanks, the coast of France stretched to the horizon in both directions. I suddenly realized that defending our position in France from an Allied invasion was going to be a huge undertaking. Unknown to me at the time, events in Berlin would soon remove me from such concerns, as Hitler announced to the German High Command his summer offensive plans for the Eastern Front, Operation Blue.

Almost without warning, our battery was ordered to pack up and return to Calais in anticipation of moving again. I bid farewell to my French hostess and her family, knowing the likely direction of our move would be eastward. As we marched to our embarkation point, I wondered if I would ever see this part of France again. By nightfall, we were speeding eastward into the night, after less than two months at Calais. One week later, the Lion awoke and launched its first thousand-bomber night raid into Europe.[9] The war was escalating.

CHAPTER 7

OPERATION BLUE

IT HAD BEEN a year since the guns of Barbarossa had awakened me on that June morning of 1941. Hitler's blitzkrieg into the Soviet Union had begun with one smashing victory after another, catching Stalin unprepared to defend against the German onslaught. While Hitler planned a victory parade in Moscow for late August, Stalin regained his composure and rallied the Soviets to fight a Great Patriotic War against the Nazi invaders, calling for scorched-earth retreat and partisan resistance behind German lines. August came and went, and Hitler had yet to ride through Red Square. Bogged down in annoying resistance skirmishes and counterattacks, the Germans conceded they had underestimated the fighting ability of the Red Army. Leningrad was encircled but had not fallen; Kiev was still holding out against incredible odds.

By September, Field Marshal von Bock was on the outskirts of Moscow with six panzer groups, poised to begin the final action of the year that would shatter the Soviet Union. Convinced the Red Army had exhausted its capacity to defend the Soviet capital, the Germans began their attack on October 2 with Operation Typhoon. Early in the campaign, it appeared Hitler's expectations of victory would come to pass as eight Soviet armies were encircled and the front was extended south to Voronezh and north to Vologda. By mid-October, however, wet autumn weather had set in, turning roads to muddy quagmires.

Though the mud slowed the attack, its effect on the Wehrmacht's overextended lines of supply was devastating. Without adequate lines of supply, pressing the attack became increasingly difficult.

When German forces broke through Mozhaisk on October 18, the Moscow defense perimeter had been breached and optimism returned in Berlin. Lenin's body was moved from its tomb to a safer location, and the government removed to Kuibyshev. Stalin remained, however, and urged the troops to redouble their efforts as they marched from the traditional October Revolution parade direct to the front. The battle raged on, and fresh Soviet troops arrived from Siberia reinforcing new lines of defense around Moscow.

On the other side of the lines the German Army threw everything it had into one final push, despite sharp disagreements between the field commanders and the German High Command. The Wehrmacht was ill prepared to fight in the winter conditions that had set in on the Moscow front. Weak lines of supply, inadequate equipment, and exhaustion had all taken their toll. On December 5, a surprise offensive strike by the Red Army broke through German lines, inflicting heavy casualties and flanking German units under orders not to retreat. By the end of December, German lines had fallen back 150 miles and the invincible reputation of blitzkrieg was over. It was a shattering defeat for the Wehrmacht.

With the entry of the United States into the war in December 1941, Germany faced the inevitability of a fight in Western Europe. Realizing he could not mount another Barbarossa, Hitler determined that a well-planned offensive in the summer of 1942 could still knock the Soviets out of the war.

* * * * * * *

As my train sped eastward from France, final preparations were being completed for Fall Blau (Code Blue), another summer offensive into the Soviet Union. Hitler had identified the major objective of Operation Blue as a push to the south to capture Stalingrad and the Caucasus oil fields. I would be taking part in the first and second phase of Operation Blue with Army Group B, which attacked eastward along the Briansk-southwest front toward Voronezh and the Don River. Phase Two entailed an encirclement move against the Red Army on the west side of the Don River. The third move would include a push toward Stalingrad. Once Stalingrad fell, a final phase was to push south to the Caucasus oil fields. The attack would begin June 28, after our arrival at the Eastern Front and full deployment of Army Group B was complete.[1]

Our train traveled through Germany and into Poland, stopping briefly in Warsaw. At the train station in Warsaw, I saw for the first time what Germans would regard as primitive facilities that were the norm throughout Eastern Europe. I had never seen such unsanitary and poorly appointed public washrooms. My friends and comrade soldiers laughed and marveled at the backward nature of the Slavs, whom we regarded as the natural opposite to German culture. As we continued east, our contempt and pity for these uncivilized people grew with each passing village and town.

Surely, these people would benefit greatly from German influence. Our superior culture and technology would bring the Slavs quickly into the twentieth century and improve their standard of living substantially. This war needed to end quickly so we could go about building new industry and commerce, an economy that would make these people thrive and appreciate German influence. My confidence in my battery and the German Army grew as I realized what we were up against. Hopefully, this mission would be over soon and we could all return home to live in peace.

Our train sped eastward through Poland and into Belorussia at Brest-Litovsk, then through the Pripet Marshes to Gomel, the last stop for our train. Gomel was an old Russian city that had been an industrial center of eastern Belorussia on the eastern side of the Dnieper River. The Soviets had succeeded in dismantling many of its industrial shops and moving them eastward when the German invasion began. Not much remained in Gomel. Everything was either destroyed or removed by the Wehrmacht.

Gomel was the end of the line for German trains whose wheelbases were built to the international gauge common to most all of Europe. At Gomel, the Russian spurs headed deeper into the Soviet Union on a much wider gauge common only to that part of the world. As the Wehrmacht pushed eastward, German Pioneer units reset the lines to a narrower gauge. When we reached Gomel, only a few lines had opened to the front, and these were reserved specifically for frontline supply. As a reinforcing unit, we began marching by foot a considerable distance from the front.

In Gomel we unloaded our horses, caissons and artillery and set out southward for Chernigov. The roads in Gomel, extending to about four miles outside of town, were bone-rattling cobblestones that jarred our teeth as we took to our "heels and wheels." The cobblestones finally ended and gave way to nothing - no roads, no highways – only directions marked by the Wehrmacht Pioneer units. We called the roads we made through the sand and dust the *Rollbahn*.

As mentioned previously, Stalin had called for strong partisan resistance behind German lines as the Red Army retreated eastward. Partisan resistance in Belorussia and the Ukraine was formidable and was manifest in a variety of forms: blown up trains, night attacks, booby traps and other hit-and-run tactics. The Russian partisans paid dearly for their resistance, most often meeting with quick and unmerciful executions if captured.

As we headed south on the *Rollbahn* to Chernigov, my battery passed many farmhouses and small villages. Some were deserted and destroyed; others showed no sign of the war that had raged through this area earlier. We feared the possibility of snipers, ambushes or other partisan attacks, and found ourselves more than once glancing over our shoulder, this way or that way, at even the slightest sound or movement.

By the end of our first day's march out of Gomel, Hauptmann von Langenstein found a suitable place to camp near some farmhouses and forest which stretched eastward to our left. As we went about setting up our camp and securing the perimeter, Russian men, women and children appeared from nowhere to watch our activities. They were friendly and seemed at ease with us, but from our perspective they seemed almost primitive. Their clothing was made from very rudimentary, hand-woven material. On one old man, I saw what appeared to be handmade moccasins made from the bark of a tree. It was obvious they were very poor and lived in conditions that apparently had not changed for several centuries.

One fellow whom I decided to call "Ivan" (after giving it much thought) was particularly interested in watching me wash the dirt and dust off my face and arms after the day's march. He was particularly friendly and fascinated with my cleansing ritual, indicating he would very much like a piece of my soap. When I gave it to him, he was delighted beyond measure and walked away with the biggest smile I had seen in months. Poor Russia! Was this the result of Stalin's vaunted efforts to bring Russians into the twentieth century with communism? Seeing these conditions, even from my limited perspective, filled me with stronger resolve that our cause was just and honorable. We needed to end this campaign quickly and decisively, and then peacefully rebuild this society into a strong, productive nation.

As nightfall came, Hauptmann von Langenstein briefed us, and the sentries were set for the night. We were all warned of the likelihood that we would encounter partisan resistance and were told, "Don't sleep too tight!"

About midnight, fireworks began as we heard shots in the trees. In the dark we scrambled for our rifles and helmets in confusing and frightening disarray. Then it was silent. After a few moments, voices were heard in the trees, a light, and then a titter of nervous laughter. Apparently a young sentry had encountered someone in the woods and, after receiving no reply when he asked for identification, had emptied his rifle into the poor soul. Further investigation revealed that he had dropped a bovine intruder in its tracks; the poor cow never knew what hit it.

Hauptmann von Langenstein assembled the battery and commended this poor embarrassed private for his bravery and fortitude. He stated that though he could not give the man an Iron Cross, he could give the battery a fine meal the next day. Relieved and somewhat amused, we retired again to our tents, knowing that nothing would penetrate our perimeter tonight. We had drawn our first blood in Russia!

* * * * * *

It was hot when I arrived in Russia; the marshes and forests were steaming with humidity that approached 100%. The horizon shimmered in the glare of the afternoon sun under a light steamy blue canopy of cloudless sky. Even the birds chose to remain in their shaded perches. The blistering heat leached every ounce of strength from my scorched body and cracked my dry, parched lips. Silently I prayed for even the slightest relief, perhaps a small cloud or, better yet, an evening shower. Even with the humidity, the dust on the *Rollbahn* had reached the consistency of fine flour and hung suspended in the suffocating, still air. It penetrated every thread of my uniform and settled in the pores of my skin. I doubted I would ever be able to clean this grime off of me. After a few days, however, I came to realize that I should not have prayed so earnestly; better I should never have prayed at all!

The summer rain finally came. It washed the dust from the air. It washed the dust from my body. It washed everything into the bottom of the *Rollbahn* where, with the help of several thousand tramping soldiers, it became the most miserable, glue- like river of mud I had ever seen. Never had I witnessed anything like the manner in which Mother Nature brought the world's finest and most powerful mechanized army to a dead halt. Our equipment was buried to the axles and solidly stuck in this most disgusting muck. I was covered in mud, from my head to my feet, covered with mud that stuck like cement. I returned to my *silent* prayers, this time asking for the return of the sun. Better to suffer dreadful heat than this mess. I only hoped my prayers this time would not be answered with such bounty as the last ones!

Finally the rains broke and we were able to move on. Gradually the *Rollbahn* dried into deep ruts with the hardness of concrete. One misstep and a twisted ankle or wrenched knee could put you out of action for several days. Gradually the ruts broke down; the hobnail boots, the horseshoes of our caisson teams, the steel tracks and the "Buna" rubber tires of the Wehrmacht recycled the *Rollbahn* to its lowest state - molecular colloidal dust suspended in steamy air.

After several days of marching, we finally reached Chernigov in the Ukraine. Hauptmann von Langenstein decided to remain there for a few days of rest before proceeding on to the front. For me, it was a welcome break that I enjoyed immensely.

Throughout our southern march to the front, we had passed several reminders of our destination. Burned-out tanks, buildings reduced to rubble and other debris from the expanding battle to the east served as constant reminders of what we were here to do.

I marveled at how rapidly the German Army had cut through the Russian defenses – it was already nearing the Volga River. As I had observed the Russian peasants along our route, I had intensified feelings of superiority and justification of the cause in which we were engaged - the liberation of these poor souls into the twentieth century. But now, as we passed the charred remains of equipment and the ugly scars of deadly battle, the signs of death were all around me. I realized again that this was not an issue of idealism; it was a struggle for life and death in its most basic form. As we lingered in Chernigov, my pride in the Wehrmacht was driven by the unrealistic hope that the Russians might surrender by the time we reached the front.

* * * * * * *

Along the *Rollbahn*, we had several opportunities to observe Russian peasants and their simple lifestyle up close. A typical village consisted of small cottages with high-peaked, thatched roofs nestled close together near a dirt road, which was their only line of communication to the outside world. Many of these villages were state-owned collective farms which had been brutally established by Stalin in the 1930s. Millions of people who had resisted the confiscation of private property and redistribution to the Soviet State had either been executed with millions of their fellow countrymen or sent to gulags in Siberia. Few of these peasants had ever ventured far from their homes, and to see armies battle through their farms was almost incomprehensible.

The most welcome sight to our battery was the typical water well in each village. The bucket suspended from its long wooden beam was lowered into the cool cistern below. The water was always refreshing and cool. Our stops at the well always gave us an opportunity to visit with these Russian peasants who were, for the most part, very friendly and anxious to talk with us.

At one stop, a Russian "Mamushka" invited me into her home for a glass of milk. As we entered the cottage, it opened into a large room where pigs, poultry, a cow and other livestock resided. From there we went through another door into a single, clay-floored room in which the entire family lived. It was here where babies were born, where children were nurtured and fed, and where grandparents died. It seemed to define the boundaries of their lives in this world.

In one corner of the room was the most prominent and most important feature – an earthen stove which was about four feet high and measured six by eight feet on the cook top. A single open fire hole in the stove allowed a cast iron pot to be placed for cooking. In another corner of the room, the woman showed me a small altar with a picture of the Virgin Mary above it. She explained to me that for years under the Stalin regime, she had hidden the icon in a wooden barrel covered with dirt. Since the invasion she had brought the altar out once more, hopefully never to be hidden again. Around the altar were framed family photographs, and as she pointed to several members of her family she would mumble one word, "Siberia."

Once again I recognized the universal basic unit of a family, just as I had in France. Once again, politics had brought disruption and turmoil to their lives. How could you explain to these humble people in any manner the reason for war? It couldn't be done. The eyes of this Mamushka were filled with sadness and hardened by the events of cruelty and injustice that had filled her life. Much of what remained dear to her was limited to a few old picture frames hanging in the dimly lit corner of a forbidden altar, erected to honor the Mother of the Prince of Peace.

* * * * * *

Hitler believed the land and resources of the Ukraine were some of the most important strategic objectives of Fall Blau. During the early stages of the 1941 campaign, Hitler had been sorely disappointed when in early July General Ewald von Kleist turned his First Panzer Group South along the Dnieper River in order to avoid urban warfare in Kiev.[2] On the cutting edge of Barbarossa, Kleist's fast-moving offensive thrust had covered almost 250 miles in two-and-a-half weeks.

By the middle of August 1941, Army Group South had closed to the Dnieper River south of Kiev. However, with only one panzer group, it had yet to complete an encirclement of Kiev. The four Russian armies defending Kiev under Lt. General M.P. Kirponos had repelled the German offensive with unexpectedly stiff resistance. In mid-August, much to the chagrin of his senior generals, Hitler ordered General Heinz Guderian and his Second Panzer Group to break off its advance on Moscow and swing south behind the Dnieper River to Kiev.

On September 16, 1941, near Rommy (120 miles east of Kiev), Guderian's Second Panzer Group linked up with Kleist's First Panzer Group coming up from the south, completing the encirclement of Kiev.[3] Still, General Kirponos had an excellent chance of breaking out. But Stalin forbade it, believing Kiev could be held. He relieved Marshal Semyon Budienny from his command over the defense of the Ukraine and appointed Marshal Semyon Timoshenko. Timoshenko arrived with barely enough time to escape by air with Budienny and the secretary of the Ukrainian Communist Central Committee, Lt. General Nikita Khrushchev, who was furious with Stalin's refusal to allow General

Kirponos to withdraw.[4] In the end, the Germans claimed to have taken 665,000 prisoners. Russian figures claimed a total of 677,085 men under Kirponos; 150,541 men escaped the encirclement and 175,000 were taken prisoner, leaving 350,000 killed in the battle for Kiev, including General Kirponos. By either account, the loss of Kiev in September 1941 had been a catastrophic defeat for the Russians. Yet, even in defeat, the Russians contributed greatly to the disruption of Hitler's timetable, which ultimately led to the Wehrmacht's failure to take Moscow.

It was almost a year later, in the hot August of 1942, when my battery marched through the ever-present cloud of dust and mosquitoes into the devastation of Kiev. The damage to the city was an incredible sight for me. Everywhere the signs of a violent struggle were seared into our consciousness as the lingering odor of decay hung in the air. At a short stop in Kiev, I noticed a church nearby and decided to take a quick look at the fabled beauty of a Russian Orthodox Church. When I swung open the huge door and gazed into the dimly lit interior, I was not prepared for what I saw. Almost every square foot of the building was covered with machinery and manufacturing equipment; steel rods connected to pulley wheels hung from the ceiling connected to other devices of this worker's perdition. I stood with my comrades in stunned silence as we beheld what had become of God in the Soviet Union. I felt as if I had mistakenly stumbled upon a dark, ugly secret; I was sick to my stomach. I wanted to run, to get away from that place before God or any of His angels found me gazing on this communist sacrilege. Again, I felt hatred for the Soviet communism that had sucked all that was good out of Russia and created this hideous, unconscionable state. Germany needed to liberate this place!

* * * * * * *

At Kiev our march turned eastward, again marching out on the bone-jarring cobblestones until we reached the *Rollbahn* and its familiar dust once more. Around us, however, the scenery was changing. We were leaving the marshy forests, mosquitoes and steamy heat, for the open steppes that stretched eastward for hundreds of miles. It was the time of the wheat harvest. But no one was there to save what was left of the crop after the men and machines had trampled through it. Beautiful sunflowers atop tall stalks hung their golden blossoms in the hot August sun. They were heavily laden with seeds that would eventually fall unharvested, much to the delight of hungry birds and rodents.

Dust was billowing up from the *Rollbahn* all the way to the horizon as we continued our relentless march to the east. The traffic began flowing in both directions as thousands and thousands of Russian POWs marched west to our prison camps. In their dirty faces I could still see the fear of their last days of fighting, the horror and shame of a battle lost. One afternoon at the end of August, we heard that General Paulus had taken Kalach on the western side of Stalingrad. We all comforted each other with the assurances that Stalingrad would soon fall.

Though September was almost upon us, the sun continued to beat down upon us with relentless heat. We began our march every morning at 7:00 a.m., while the cool air allowed us to make good time. By noon, however, the going would become slow and exhausting under a cloudless sky. We all feared the exposure to a possible enemy air attack that fortunately never came. Around us the burned hulks of tanks and trucks marked the defeat of the Russians at this same place one year earlier. We asked ourselves continually, "How long can Stalin last with these staggering losses?"

One morning four *zugmaschinen* (tracked personnel carriers) arrived, asking for Hauptmann von Langenstein. After a brief meeting, we were informed that our heavy guns were needed at the front. We hooked the howitzers to the vehicles and climbed aboard for the last stretch of *Rollbahn* to the front, which was little more than a day away. It felt wonderful to ride.

Late the following afternoon we stopped near a wooded hill. We jumped from the troop carrier and scrambled to the top of the hill, from which we could see the front line about three miles away. We were able to see and hear the artillery fire in the distance. A chill came over me as I realized that we were finally at the front. I was staring death in the face, knowing that the time had now come for me to focus on surviving against a ruthless, godless enemy.

After a short briefing, Hauptmann von Langenstein jumped into a Opel and ordered me to bring my men and follow him. As the sun dipped in the west, a cool breeze hinting the coming of autumn ruffled the heat from the afternoon air. We followed von Langenstein's Opel ever closer to the front, where our observation post would be located.

It was dark when we finally started digging in. I sent three men to establish the phone connection to the firebase and the rest of us dug trenches. Our infantry line was not more than 500 yards in front of us, and beyond the infantry were the Russians. Once in a while the sky would light up under a flare, which lasted only a few moments, and then it would be dark again. Just after midnight we quit digging and fell exhausted into our foxholes. The moment I had thought about for months had arrived, but not even the excitement and danger of what lay a scant quarter of a mile away could hold my attention long. Within a few minutes I was fast asleep.

CHAPTER 8

THE EASTERN FRONT

BEFORE DAWN ON my first day of battle on the Eastern Front, I received a rude wake-up call from five Russian YAK-9D fighter planes. They were firing their 12.7mm machine guns at the infantry positions in front of us. They were coming in about 200 feet above the ground on a strafing run directly toward our foxholes. I didn't bother to get a good look, choosing instead to study the floor of my foxhole up close! As the planes roared over our position, I heard the familiar hum of the faster, more powerful ME-109G whining up from the west. The YAKs suddenly broke to the right in a quick turn back toward the Russian lines. In only a few moments, they each began to explode and fall from the sky, 20mm tracers from the Messerschmidts piercing through their wide underbellies. At 200 feet above the ground, it only took a moment before each unfortunate pilot crashed in a huge ball of flame and curling black smoke. None of the Russian pilots survived.

The surgical precision of these German fighters was both awesome to behold and frightening to think about. War on the Eastern Front made no concessions to inexperience or inferior firepower. If either side made a concession, the other would take advantage without hesitation. The object of this fight was to kill. Of all the considerations given by thinking men on this front, human life mattered the least. As I stood in the predawn light of that July morning, watching the last vestiges of five human lives roil up in black clouds of burning fuel and wreckage, I knew that death had now become an unwelcome guest, an intruder that was not likely to go away.

Within a few minutes, the familiar voice of Hauptmann von Langenstein spoke reassuringly from above the trench. Satisfied with our evening's work, he told us that we needed more trenches for all the men who would occupy the position. After a quick breakfast, we grabbed our shovels and went back to work setting up our *B-Stelle*. Later in the morning, the *Sheren-Fernrohr* (range finder) arrived and, with the communications line open to the *Feuerstellung* (fire base), we were ready to commence firing.

Hauptmann von Langenstein stepped to the range finder and began twisting knobs. A smile broke over his face as he reported, "I can't see any Russians!" They were fleeing to the east in retreat. Taking out his map, he studied it closely before again stepping to the range finder. Checking his map, he commented, "The Russians must be using this village for cover. Let's see what happens if we send a few rounds here," pointing to a position on the chart. A call was made to the firebase, and our first firing command was made:

"*Funfsten Ladung Aufschlag!* (Load fifth powder charge!)

Ganze Battery! (Entire battery!)

Von Grundrichtung funf und dreizig mehr . . . (From the ground reference point thirty-five [degrees] to the right . . .)

Funf und neunzig hunderd . . . (Ninety-five hundred [range])

Feuer bereitschaft melden!" (Report when ready to fire!)

The battery reported it was ready.

"FEUER!"

Hauptmann von Langenstein, his eyes glued to the eyepiece, broke into another grin a few moments later.

"Donnerwetter!"

A direct hit. Tanks were rolling out of the village in every direction. Black smoke curled above the village indicating that hits had been made. A new call to the firebase increased the range and ordered 30 rounds per gun to fire for effect. As the artillery rained down on the fleeing Russian tanks, some disappeared in clouds of gray smoke and flash, leaving a burning hulk when the dust cleared. It was too far away to see the effect on Russian soldiers, but we knew that our firebase had rained high explosive shells on several Russians who could not have survived. Watching the real effects of what I had trained for over the past 13 months was sobering, but I had to put it out of my mind. Stalin's artillery batteries would be pleased to rain the same death on Germans, whether we had invaded or not.

By midmorning the infantry was on the move again, chasing after the retreating Russians. We packed our gear, rolled up the communications lines, and followed the front as it expanded eastward. Thus began our routine for the next few weeks as we followed the demoralized Red Army eastward through the Donets Corridor to the southwestern side of the Don River, where it turns eastward from its southerly course near Pavlovsk.

On some days we would retrench, fire our guns, then move again for a second artillery barrage in the afternoon. The late summer sun continued to beat down on us; fierce heat, smoke, dust and the smell of war clogged every pore and sapped our bodies of all the energy we could muster.

Despite the harsh conditions on the Don front, I was still grateful that I was not a part of the highly mobile panzer divisions at Stalingrad. True, being attached to an infantry division limited our mobility; however, this disadvantage was far more agreeable than fighting fanatical Russians who were defending Stalingrad from house to house.

* * * * * * *

German soldiers had been in Russia for over a year, and had already been turned back at Moscow. The Russians believed strongly the German Army would eventually be driven from their homeland. The 1942 offensive raised new concerns over the defense of Mother Russia, as Stalin now chose to characterize his Soviet nation, and the cry for defense of the homeland reached new levels of nationalistic fervor. Still, the Russians could not stop our surge to the Don. In the face of defeat after defeat, the Red Army began to collapse, having no semblance of order or discipline. Further to the southwest, the city of Rostov had fallen in late July, opening the way for Field Marshal Wilhelm List's drive into the Caucasus. With the fall of Rostov, Russian morale hit an all-time low. Most Russians were savvy enough to realize that if the Wehrmacht took the oil and mineral-rich Caucasus and Stalingrad, the war would, in effect, be over.

Arriving at the Don front from his diplomatic post in China in early July, General Chuikov observed conditions that he later described in his memoirs in grim detail:

> I saw how these people were moving along the waterless Stalingrad Steppe from west to east, eating their last reserves of food, and overcome by the stifling heat. When I asked them, "Where are you going? Who are you looking for?" they gave senseless answers. They all seemed to be looking for somebody on the other side of the Volga, or in the Saratov region. . . In the steppe, I met the staffs of two divisions who claimed to be looking for the H.Q. of the 9th Army. These staffs consisted of a few officers sitting in three or four cars, loaded to the brim with petrol tins. In reply to my questions, "Where are the Germans? Where are our units? Where are you going?" they didn't know what to say.[1]

Stirred by the gallant, though unsuccessful, defense of Sebastopol, which had fallen on July 2, and equally angry at the wholesale retreat of the Red Army, Stalin vowed the city that bore his name would not fall. On July 28, he issued his famous "Not a Step Back" order, which turned out to be more literal than figurative. The order did, however, mark a major turning point for the Red Army, with a drastic overhaul in order and discipline and ruthless punishment for cowardice and disobedience. Soldiers who disobeyed or deserted faced summary executions or assignment to front-line positions that most certainly would result in death.

Noted historian Alexander Werth has described a threefold reformation in the officer corps of the Red Army during this period that would eventually have a significant effect in turning the tide of defeat into victory.[3] "Old war horses" were promoted up and off the front, leaving room for the promotion of younger, more experienced, capable officers to command front-line troops. Second, for the first time since the Bolshevik Revolution, officers wore new, distinctive uniforms and were awarded new medals for valor, named for old Russian Heroes; the Orders of Suvorov, Kutuzov and Nevsky. Quite literally, says Werth, "out of the flames of Stalingrad" would emerge the gold-braided officer corps of the Red Army.[4]

Finally, and perhaps most significantly, the dual command structure between the army officer and party commissar was scrapped in favor of singular command for army officers. By 1942, Stalin determined the need for party commissars to oversee old, untrustworthy Tsarist Army officers had outgrown its purpose. While many foreign diplomats scoffed at these obvious cosmetic changes to Red Army organization,

Stalin counted heavily on his new officer corps. He needed it to stem the tide of crumbling morale and slow the German advance enough to buy him the time needed to reinforce Stalingrad and the Don front.

In Berlin, Hitler had been furious with the slow progress of our advance and ordered Stalingrad to be taken by August 25. On August 23, the Luftwaffe launched a massive air attack with 600 bombers on the encircled city that resulted in the death of more than 40,000 Russian civilians. Still, the Russians held, much to the consternation of Hitler. When a report was given stating that Stalin could possibly muster more than a million fresh troops for the Don front and another half million in the Caucasus, Hitler flew at the officer with fists clenched in rage, literally foaming at the corners of his mouth. He ordered him not to read any more idiotic twaddle.[5] When General Franz Halder pointed out that it did not require the gift of a prophet to foresee what would happen if Stalin unleashed one and a half million men on the Don and Stalingrad fronts, Hitler dismissed him as Chief of the Army General Staff.[6]

As a line soldier at the front, I had no knowledge of the organizational problems and morale of the Red Army, and was equally ignorant of the motives and strategy of Hitler and the German High Command. I was a Prussian soldier fighting in the German Army, just as my father had, and his father had. I was a highly trained part of the most powerful, best-equipped army the world had ever seen. My view was purely tactical and was seldom wider than the field of my spotting glasses. I carried out my duties to the best of my ability and obeyed the orders of my superiors without question. I was proud of the efficiency of my battery and equally proud of the overwhelming might of the German army. It was not my place to question why I was in Russia. I was a German fighting soldier at war with the hated communists and the ruthless dictator Stalin whose totalitarian regime had murdered millions in the years of collectivization. Stalin and communism had kept Russia in the dark ages too long. Clearly, the Russians could only benefit from what Germany had to offer. My outlook may not have been complete and was perhaps oversimplified, but most other young German soldiers on the Eastern Front shared it nevertheless.

In August, as panic among the Russians subsided into the dull ache of fear, a new emotion began growing among the Russian people. It was a feeling that began to permeate all of Russia as it struggled against the Nazi invaders.[7] Poets, writers and musicians began to weave an artistic pattern of hatred toward the Germans in works that swept through Russia with a religious fervor.[8] On August 12, Alexei Surkov published his poem, *I Hate* which ended with the lines:

> My heart is hard as stone,
> My grievances and memories are countless,
> With these hands of mine
> I have lifted corpses of little children . . .
> I hate them deeply
> For those hours of sleepless gloom.
> I hate them because in one year
> My temples have grown white.
> My house has been defiled by the Prussians,
> Their drunken laughter dims my reason.

And with these hands of mine
I want to strangle every one of them.[9]

As we advanced into the Don Bend and German troops entered the
outskirts of Stalingrad, Ilya Ehrenburg wrote in the *Red Star*:

> ... One can bear anything; the plague, and hunger and
> death. But one cannot bear the Germans. One cannot
> bear these fish-eyed oafs contemptuously snorting at
> everything Russian. . . We cannot live as long as these
> gray-green slugs are alive. Today there are no books;
> today there are no stars in the sky; today there is only
> one thought; Kill the Germans. Kill them all and dig
> them into the earth. Then we can go to sleep. Then we
> can think again of life, and books, and girls, and
> happiness. . . Let us not rely on rivers and mountains.
> We can only rely on ourselves. Thermopylae did not
> stop them. Nor did the Sea of Crete. Men stopped
> them, not in the mountains, but in the suburban
> allotments of Moscow. We shall kill them all. But we
> must do it quickly; or they will desecrate the whole of
> Russia and torture to death millions more people.[10]

My comrades and I were unaware of the propaganda and
nationalistic pride that was reinvigorating the Red Army. Our reception
in Belorussia and the Ukraine led many of us to believe that we were
liberators of the Russian Volk, not conquerors. We continued the
relentless work of war, fighting at the front in unbearable heat, dust and
smoke. At times it seemed impossible to do all that was required and
still keep sharp and stay alive. We hated communism but could not
project that hate onto the Russian people. They were victims, not of the

Wehrmacht, but of the despot Stalin who kept them in ignorance. We had no time to hate Russians. We feared what the Red Army could do to us if we slipped in any of our responsibilities. Though Stalin's soldiers appeared beaten, they could still kill, and the only way we could prevent that was to do our job better than they did theirs.

* * * * * * *

Through the end of July and into August, we pushed deeper into the Don Bend. The Red Army seemed to fight harder as we got closer to the river, and our progress slowed. Ahead of us, billowing clouds of dust marked the movement of Russian troops and equipment. Between our position and the dust clouds left by the Russians, German infantry moved cautiously ahead.

When the Russians reached the Don River north of the German bridgehead at Vertyachiy, they turned to face us, digging in on the south and western side. Since our objective was not to cross the Don north of the bridgehead, we closed the Russian lines by early August and began to dig in to hold the 6th Army's long left flank. To the south, General Paulus and his motorized divisions reached the edge of Stalingrad. Fierce fighting had commenced from street to street.

Faced with the difficult task of protecting a long and exposed northern flank, we quickly set about building a defensive line. All of us dug and dug. We built trenches and bunkers and watched the enemy carefully through our binoculars and rangefinders. They too were

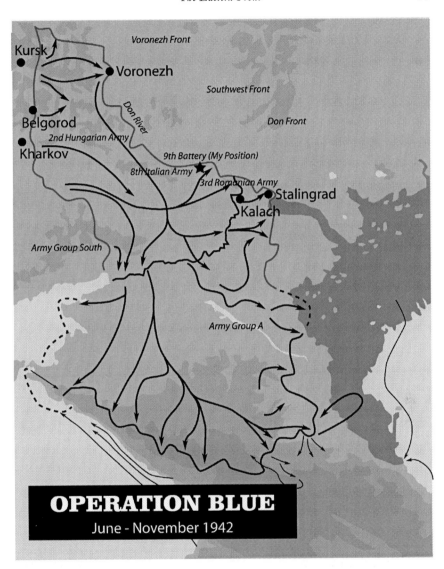

Kursk

Voronezh Front

Voronezh

Southwest Front

Belgorod

Don River

Don Front

2nd Hungarian Army

Kharkov

9th Battery (My Position)

8th Italian Army

3rd Romanian Army

Stalingrad

Kalach

Army Group South

Army Group A

OPERATION BLUE

June - November 1942

digging in. Though it remained warm into early September, we knew the Russians would soon be reinforced by their old ally, "General Winter" who had more than once defeated Russian enemies with blasts of cold air and furious winter storms. We prepared as best we could, digging three lines of defenses and an intricate network of fortified bunkers where we could stay warm and dry.

As both sides settled in, the exchange of fire increased. Explosions and flying shrapnel took their toll, and the number of German casualties increased. Over the next several weeks I was asked to assume more responsibilities, even though I was still relatively inexperienced. On one occasion I was sent out with Wachtmeister Erlich to the forward observation post for on-the-job training as a spotter for our big guns. Before the war, he had been a judge in Königsburg. I will never forget him. I learned more about the law than about being a forward observer, and had to laugh because he was always lost.

After we completed our fortifications, a new antitank gun arrived and was placed near my bunker at the *B-Stelle*. It was a good position for the gun, but I was not pleased. It would become a primary target for Russian artillery. I was more than happy to take my position at the forward observation post with the infantry during our weekly rotation. Even though I was only 100 yards away from the Russian front lines, I felt safer. All I could see through my field glasses were mounds of dirt, which marked the forward Russian trench. I seldom saw any Russian soldiers, and even then only caught brief glimpses.

I came to appreciate and respect the life of an infantry soldier who had to fight under all conditions and do the best he could when no replacements arrived for the growing number of casualties. They lived under constant pressure, but were nevertheless fun to be with. They felt safe with an artillery spotter, and I never let on that my inexperience might give them cause for concern.

After a week with the infantry, I returned to the firebase. If the front was calm, it would have been a week of rest, cleanup and letter writing. Though we worked hard to remain clean, we were still overwhelmed with lice. They were everywhere! Residing in our beds of straw and in our clothing, these bloodsuckers never let up; it was disgusting. Nothing was more revolting than having to deal with lice. As if bullets and shrapnel were not enough, these miserable creatures were capable of taking you out with typhus.

The week on the hill at the *B-Stelle* was much more interesting. From our viewpoint, we could see the Russian lines clearly, and even their installations behind the lines. We recorded all of our observations in logbooks and noted every suspicious movement. One afternoon in late September I watched a field of huge Russian sunflowers that had grown to heights of seven and eight feet. I had a feeling that eventually we might see something moving out of that field and made a note to that effect in the logbook. The next morning, Hauptmann von Langenstein decided the field might indeed be a good hiding place for Russian T-34 tanks. He called for support from other batteries, and together we commenced a withering barrage of *Abpraller,* or ricocheting ammunition. *Abpraller* ammunition consisted of grenade explosives that were set with a delayed fuse. After the grenade hit the ground, it exploded deadly shrapnel 30 to 40 feet in the air.

As barrage after barrage of *Abpraller* ammunition started hitting the field of sunflowers, it soon turned into a hornet's nest. Russian tanks came roaring out of the field at full speed headed for our infantry lines. One by one, our new 75mm antitank guns began destroying Russian tanks. Some tanks hit mines. Others got stuck, becoming a sure target for antitank guns, which methodically found their range and then blew the tanks to pieces.

Still the Russian attack pressed forward and our infantry fell back. Our firebase trenches became the first line of defense. I felt strange knowing that our position was now the target of most every tank in the field. Nothing in the previous few months had compared with this free-for-all of intensive and deadly fire. To our left, more Russian tanks were breaching our lines and were coming within 500 yards of our hill. The antitank gun near my bunker became a key to our defense. Uffz. Brinkman coolly called site and distance to each target, and with a huge reddish-yellow explosion, another Russian tank would erupt into flaming chunks of steel and death, scattering across the battlefield. There was no time to cheer, as yet another tank would roll forward out of the smoke, only to disappear in another explosion of burned steel and flesh.

Seeing the tide had turned, the Russian tanks retreated. Almost as quickly as it began, it was over. Uffz. Brinkman had accounted for an astonishing 24 destroyed tanks. We were stunned and suddenly very pleased with our new weapon. I was spellbound at the sight in front of me: a wide vista of burning hulks, scarred landscape and dead soldiers under huge clouds of burning diesel fuel.

As the smoke cleared, I suddenly realized there were ten Russian soldiers standing in front of us. They pushed their rifles into the ground and raised their arms in surrender. I motioned for them to keep their arms raised and jump down into the trench. One of them spoke fairly good German and became their spokesman. We offered them food and drink, which they gladly accepted. I noticed that two of them were women.

I was reassured to see the infantry below us, moving back to our original front line. I wondered how many of my friends had survived, and who would not be there when I next rotated to the front line.

As I sat in the late afternoon sun with our newly captured Russian prisoners, all of us covered with sweat and dirt, I began to talk casually to their leader. I learned he was from Odessa on the Black Sea, where he had been a teacher. He believed that Stalin was finished and was terribly afraid of the NKVD who had been ordered to execute all "traitors" on the spot, which could apply without warning to anyone. He told me that his reserve unit had arrived only a few days earlier and that no one in his unit had been issued a rifle. The party commissars told him that he would find a rifle at the front, on a dead comrade.

He looked at my uniform and shook his head at how well equipped his German foes were, compared to his shabby, dirty uniform. Over his shoulder he carried a worn bag, which held ammunition, a chunk of stale bread and a cube of rancid bacon. I asked him how he could eat such food, to which he responded, "When you're hungry, it tastes like honey," words that would come to haunt me in the not-too-distant future.

As I looked to the west, into the reddish hues of a smoky, setting sun, I suddenly felt an overwhelming sensation of gratitude that I was still alive. The enormity of this day's experience hit me hard as I looked at the burning tanks surrounded by dead Russian and German soldiers, and then at my Russian prisoners, in whose eyes I could see pain, fear and relief. At a loss for words, I just stood for a while and tried to comprehend this experience, to take it all into my memory for a time someday when I might be able to understand.

I turned back to my new Russian friend and asked if he would join the Russian forces who were fighting with the Germans under the Russian General Andrei Vlassov.[11] He looked down, then away at the burning tanks. He said nothing. I knew it was a hard question, so I didn't press the issue. He and his comrades stayed with us a few more days and helped dig trenches. Then we bid farewell as he was escorted with other prisoners to the rear, headed for some unknown location to the west. I had no idea what would become of him.

CHAPTER 9
HOME AGAIN

IN OCTOBER THE weather changed. Cold winds from the north combined with rain to make life miserable on the Eastern Front. The roads turned to mud and became impassable. Though we were uncomfortable and inconvenienced by the onset of unseasonable winter-like weather, it did bring a lull in the fighting. Visibility through the range finder was limited. When we did get a good look, it appeared the Russians were also lying low. In reality, however, our unscientific observations could not have been further from the truth.

Since the massive bombing of Stalingrad by the Luftwaffe on August 23, its continued defense by the Red Army astonished all of us. Though the Russians had continued to suffer heavy losses through September, they had forced the Wehrmacht to pay dearly for every floor in every building on every block taken in Stalingrad. As the Russians retreated deeper and deeper into the hellish caldron, their resistance became legend throughout the Soviet Union. It was a rallying point needed by General Chuikov to inspire a stand by the Red Army and to put into effect the final defense of Stalingrad, a counteroffensive code-named Uranus.

* * * * * *

One evening in early November I stepped outside our bunker to watch the onset of a howling storm falling on us from the north. There wasn't much to see, but the sting of the blizzard blowing over this forsaken corner of the Russian steppes struck fiercely against my face. An occasional flare would rocket into the pitch-black night, only to have its light flicker and disappear into a swirling, howling mass of frozen sleet.

It seemed that whenever I felt alone and exposed to the ravages of man and nature, Hauptmann von Langenstein would appear from nowhere. He always had a grin on his face and the pockets of his leather trench coat were invariably filled with treats for his men. Standing more than six feet tall, his dark hair and brown eyes bespoke firmness and deep confidence. He commanded undying loyalty from all of his men, who would have gladly followed him to the gates of Hell, as we seemingly had already done. All of us knew that behind his stern, exacting leadership was a warm human being with genuine love and concern for all of us. It was on nights such as this that he would spend long periods of time with each of his men, giving words of encouragement, discussing personal problems and keeping up with families and loved ones back home.

When Hauptmann von Langenstein found me, it was too cold to stay outside. So we returned to a quiet bunker, lit only by candles. Someone was monitoring technical equipment and several phone lines, which were normally quiet at night. The rest of my men were either writing home to family and loved ones or keeping thoughts to themselves. The only exception was one standing next to the stove as naked as a jaybird. He had declared war on the lice that had infested his bunk, his clothes and his whole being! He stood patiently, picking them off one by one and tossing them into an open can heating over a candle. He took great satisfaction in knowing the lice were suffering for the crimes they had committed against his body over the last several weeks.

Though the blizzard howled outside, inside we were warm. All of us had been issued new reversible white and gray winter outerwear, but inside the bunker we hardly needed it. In one corner of our cozy shelter stood one of our most important pieces of equipment, a crude stove topped with a steel plate from a shattered Russian tank. Simple in design, our stove kept us warm throughout the night. The armor plate that had failed its former owners now served us well. It radiated heat throughout the bunker and doubled as a toaster to warm bread and rations.

After Hauptmann von Langenstein had a moment with each of my men, he gathered us together. He told us a new officer had arrived to relieve him and that, after a brief visit home to Hamburg, he would be moving on. The news of his reassignment saddened us. We hoped fate would perhaps bring us together again soon. As it turned out, I would be the only one who would ever see him again, two years later, on the Eastern Front in Poland.

* * * * * * *

The following morning it was again my turn to rotate to the front line trenches with the infantry. There were new faces as well as many friends I had come to know over the last several weeks.

Early in the morning after my arrival, I awoke from a deep slumber to the sound of the field telephone ringing in our outpost. It was von Langenstein calling from the firebase to tell me that I was going home for a month-long vacation. Within a few minutes, I was packed and eagerly awaiting my replacement. Home to Tilsit! I couldn't believe my good fortune to be out of this lice-infested icebox. Even though it was still early November, snow and ice were beginning to collect across the steppes. These early blizzards were only a hint of what was soon to come.

It did not take me long to get to the firebase, and from there I walked to the support base where I caught a bus the next morning to Kastornoye. After another cold night on the straw- covered floor of the barracks in Kastornoye, I boarded a train the next afternoon for Gomel, our first stop in the return to civilization. We were told not to sleep and to keep our boots on and rifles ready in case partisans attacked our train. The prospect of danger, together with the gloomy overcast day, still could do nothing to dampen my spirits. Staying awake was not a problem.

At Gomel we had to strip off all of our clothing for delousing. They literally baked our uniforms to kill all the parasites. Crossing a long wooden bridge into the "clean" camp, I again boarded a train, this one bound for Königsburg. I was a new man! It felt incredibly good to be back in familiar surroundings.

Once I arrived in Tilsit, I quickly put the front behind me. It was difficult for me to describe the horrors of war to my family and friends. My mother looked shocked when I asked her to boil my underwear to ensure no lice had survived the trip.

For three weeks I enjoyed the theater, opera, restaurants, movies and friends. One evening I ran into a cousin who was also home from the war. He was a U-boat sailor with fascinating stories about his adventures on the high seas. One particular story captured my imagination as he described looking through the periscope at the night lights of New York City. For both of us the war seemed so far away, and home was so comfortable. Unfortunately, time passed too quickly.

As my furlough drew to a close, ominous news began to appear in the newspapers and over the evening news broadcasts. The situation on the Russian front, especially near Stalingrad, was worsening. Then, early in the morning of November 19, it happened. The Russian 5th Tank Army and 21st Army blew through the remnants of the Rumanian 3rd Army, which had only moments before been annihilated by a withering artillery barrage.[1] In a matter of days the Russians moved southwest toward Kalach, and there, on November 22, they completed the encirclement of Stalingrad. General Vatutin connected with General Yeremenko, who had driven north from his breakthrough to the south

of Stalingrad. The encirclement trapped General Paulus and almost a quarter of a million soldiers of the German 6th Army.[2]

While these developments shocked me, I was not surprised. As I listened to the grim news from the front, I reflected on my observations of Rumanian troops who had guarded our southern flank on the Don front. To many of us they were a joke. Their artillery and rifles were of World War I vintage. None of these soldiers were eager to be deep in Russia fighting a war they did not think was theirs. Now they were gone, and our southern flank lay open. The Russians had broken through the weakest point of the front, and, ironically, the retreating soldiers had fallen back to the safety of Stalingrad. Now, it was only a matter of time.

The radio broadcast ordered all Eastern Front soldiers on leave to report to the nearest military authority. Reporting in Tilsit, I was told that no one was sure how bad the situation really was, but I would have eight more days in Tilsit before returning to the front.

* * * * * * *

The mood was somber on the train returning to the front. About 200 soldiers were crowded into each car of the long train that sped eastward through the night at almost 80 mph. Outside, a deep blanket of snow covered the landscape. Those on the train said little. Many of the soldiers slept; others sat in the darkness keeping their thoughts to themselves. I did not have a bench, so I sat on my pack and leaned against the rocking bulkhead, my gun ready, too terrified to sleep.

As we approached the Pripet Marshes, everyone was awakened and told to stay alert. Russian partisans had been planting mines on the railroad tracks almost every night. For almost 75 miles we rushed through a landscape of twisted wreckage and burned-out train cars. Ahead of the locomotive, two flatbed cars ran point for the train. The hope was the cars would detonate any mines, thus minimizing casualties. It was hard to imagine that casualties could be light in a train derailed at 80 mph.

Hitler had promised General Paulus that he would airlift food and supplies to the divisions trapped in Stalingrad. However, the bitter winter that had descended across the Eastern Front had prevented the

Luftwaffe from supplying the bases at Pitomik and Gumrak on a regular basis; the airlift could not help. It seemed certain to most of us that we were rushing straight into the jaws of death.

It was early in the morning when our train finally stopped. Military police boarded the train to ensure that everyone got off. They told us it was impossible to return to our units, and that all of us were to board the trucks ahead of the train, which would take us to the front. As I watched the chaos unfold, I had a feeling that something was wrong. A few others and I quietly worked our way to the edge of the crowd and disappeared into the confusion to search for our units. Within 48 hours I found the 9th Battery, still entrenched where I had left it less than a month earlier.

* * * * * * *

A week after Christmas it was my turn to take the forward observer position on the front line. Shortly after sundown in the late afternoon of January 3, 1943, I set out with four others for the infantry bunker. I expected to be there about a week, our normal rotation period. The snow was deep and the clear night extremely cold. It took us an hour to reach the bunker. After arriving and reporting to the firebase by phone, I was immediately ordered to gather everyone and return at once. Quickly, we rounded up our gear and destroyed what we could not carry. As we hurried back, I noticed for the first time the trenches were empty. A chill of fear seized me as I realized the infantry had fallen back. Were we behind enemy lines? When we reached the firebase, my unit had destroyed all but one of our howitzers. In the midst of pandemonium and confusion, the evacuation had started. We were falling back, and the grim faces of experienced soldiers revealed that our situation was serious.

Unknown to me at the time, several divisions under General Vatutin and General Golikov had pushed into the Don country from the north as part of Operation Saturn. The Russians had driven south and west through the Italian 8th and Hungarian 2nd Army toward Kharkov. When von Manstein's effort to break through to Stalingrad failed, more Russian troops in the south were now able to move north and west to encircle our position. We were trapped with no line of supply. Only the senior officers knew the full extent of our predicament, and they were keeping it to themselves.

Shortly after midnight, our battery commander gave us the word to move out. We headed west into the bitterly cold night, the moon eerily casting our shadows across the barren snowscape. Where were the Russians? Though all of us felt we were being watched, we saw no sign of the enemy.

We trudged all night through the deep snow under a brilliant canopy of bright stars. We spoke little. All of us knew the Russians would be merciless in any confrontation, and the road for all prisoners would most certainly end in the gulags of Siberia. Under such circumstances, death would be a more desirable fate.

As the gray light of early dawn widened our view, a few small villages appeared out of the haze. Later, we reached the main road over which we had come eastward only four months earlier. More soldiers joined us from the Don Front, and for the moment I felt more secure in company with larger numbers. We marched on through the afternoon. By nightfall we had found shelter in a small village. Still there was no sign of the Russians.

Our kitchen chef was able to put together a hot meal. Later in the evening, the group leaders gathered with our battery commander in a small peasant farmhouse. Lit by a single kerosene lamp, the room was still quite dim as the captain unfolded the map on the table. With a clinical, monotonous tone he explained the collapse of the Italian 8th Army and the Hungarian 2nd Army on our northern flank. The front was now open between Voronezh and Stalingrad, a distance of roughly 350 kilometers. It was unlikely that reserve units would ever reinforce our position. Indeed, he explained, we were surrounded by the Russian Army.

The captain believed our chances of breaking through the Russian lines were good. Showing deep emotion only once, he spoke quietly of reunion with our families in our homeland. The severity of our situation, however, required us to abandon the last Howitzer and stay close together, armed only with our rifles.

As the meeting broke up, it was close to midnight on another bitterly cold, clear night. When he walked out of the hut, several men surrounded the captain asking questions for which he had no answers. Mounting his horse, he stood in the saddle and called out to all the men in a firm, strong voice, "*Rette sich wer kann!*" ("every man for himself!") Drawing his pistol from his holster, he laid it against his temple and pulled the trigger. In stunned silence we watched his lifeless body slide from the saddle and land in a crumpled heap in the snow. After a few moments to collect ourselves, we quietly wrapped his body in a blanket and buried him where he fell. We were now on our own.

Many officers and men fled immediately. I was responsible for a group of 10 men who all gathered around me. We decided to stay together and survive as a team. We resolved to fill our pockets with as much ammunition as we could carry and to share in the responsibility of finding food for all. After destroying all of our remaining equipment we set out in a westerly direction.

Scanning the heavens, I quickly identified Ursa Minor, "the Little Dipper", with Polaris at the end of its tail. Keeping it to our right, I knew we would be heading west.

Pushing on into the night, I believed that my life would most likely end soon, but I resolved not to give up. With every last fiber of my being I would fight to survive and return to my homeland, my family, and my friends. I knew that my faith in God would support me and that He would be with me no matter what happened. For the next three months, that knowledge was the only comfort and strength I would have.

CHAPTER 10
RETREAT

ALL OF US have grown from childhood with a folklore image of Hell as flames, brimstone and heat. As I marched westward with the men of the 9th Battery in early January 1943, I learned first-hand that Hell was snow, ice, bitterly cold wind and sleet, frozen bodies in grotesque form, little food and no sleep.

After we had destroyed our equipment and loaded our pockets with ammunition, we had no need to wait for dawn. We marched all night in temperatures close to -40 degrees Celsius. The crunching of our boots over the snow reminded me of squeezing a box of cornstarch. This night there was no wind, only the sound of men marching into the dark gloom of the western horizon.

We had a horse that pulled a sled, on which we had placed all of our individual gear. Because it was so cold, I decided that no one could ride on the sled. We needed to keep walking to keep warm and to keep blood flowing to our extremities. Even that could not prevent the onset of frostbite, but it was the best we could do.

One afternoon on the second or third day of our march, one of the soldiers in my group named Rockel came to me and begged me to let him ride on the sled. He was so tired and worn out, he didn't think he could take another step. I warned him that it was too dangerous and encouraged him to keep walking. A few moments later, he sat down on the sled and leaned against the equipment. Within a half hour, his head drooped and he was gone. All we could do was pull him off the sled and lay him in the snow. Within a week, all of my comrades in the 9th Battery had drifted off, frozen to death, or become lost. I would only see one of them again, several weeks later as I walked through a Russian village. Though I constantly looked for them over the next several weeks and months, I never found any more of them.

Some soldiers in the column were so weak they would simply lie down in the snow and go to sleep, never to awaken again. Others received wounds in firefights and then, already starving, lacked the strength to keep moving. There was little, if any, medical aid available. A fortunate few found a place on larger horse-drawn sleds with blankets and straw that could shelter them from the cold. Lacking feed, however, even some of the horses soon lost their strength. More than one animal found itself on the menu for starving soldiers.

More men continued to join our column as we moved along the *Rollbahn*. Its dust was now frozen solid under the snow-covered steppes, beneath the concrete-like ruts that would not thaw for several more months. Despite our predicament, I felt secure in numbers. Nevertheless, I think all of us realized that it was, indeed, every man for himself. All of us would help our comrades in arms, but we knew that survival would depend on our own will to live. We had to keep our wits about us. Once in a while, you could feel the panic swell inside you.

With considerable effort you had to force it back down. Fear was a constant companion; it kept you alert. Panic, however, could be deadly.

We thought constantly about possibilities - *what will I do if an attack comes from our flank? * Or *where can I take cover if an attack comes at this moment?* When I was not thinking about these possibilities, I thought about the enemy. I reminded myself the Russians would show me no mercy. My crusading idealism had faded in the blinding light of reality. I was an invader; I had come into their land; their homes were gone; their family and friends had been killed. Had our efforts succeeded, maybe they would have seen us as the liberators we had fancied ourselves as we marched through Belorussia and the Ukraine the summer before. Now we had failed. They hated us more than evil itself. I doubted seriously they would even take us as prisoners. As a prisoner, my life would only be prolonged in agony, to end somewhere in Siberia, if I even made it that far.

The *Rollbahn* was a thick column of men that appeared to stretch from horizon to horizon, moving forward like an undulating snake. Abandoned and damaged trucks lay along the roadside. Some of them contained supplies and mail that would never be delivered. Searching through these trucks we found packages of food, cookies and bonbons meant for soldiers on the front. I stuffed my pockets full of anything and everything I could find. It quickly became clear that food was more important than ammunition.

We were so exhausted and cold that I doubted that any of us could mount an effective defense if we were attacked. My rifle became more useful as a walking stick than a weapon. Gradually I rationalized that if there were a battle, I would probably need only a handful of ammunition. I didn't expect to last very long.

All of us knew the reality of our situation. Pondering it could have two effects - either it would discourage you and eventually you'd give up, or it would motivate you to keep moving and never give up. For me, it was the latter. I resolved deep in my soul that I would keep going as long as I had an ounce of energy left to expend – one foot in front of the other, stopping only to rest. If there was one chance in a billion for me to see my home again, then I wanted that chance. If I gave up, then there was no chance.

Though we headed west the first few days and weeks, our path did not always continue in the same direction. Almost every day there would be fighting, as we would come upon a Russian perimeter, or we would encounter a Russian patrol. It was not our goal to engage the enemy. We wanted only to escape. Sometimes we would turn south; other times we would swing east and back to the north.

Sometimes we moved only when it was light; other times we walked all night. The sun set about 3:00 p.m., after which the temperature would plummet. If it was stormy, the sky would simply get dark and stay that way until around 9:00 a.m. the next morning.

At night we came upon fires along the *Rollbahn*. There was plenty to burn - truck tires, broken rifle stocks, debris from supply trucks. A red glow in the distance usually marked a burning farm or village. Many soldiers chose to avoid fires and the warmth they provided simply because of the excellent target you became as you warmed your feet, silhouetted by the fire. Sometimes we came upon a deserted village, with buildings badly damaged, and roofs or walls caved in, framing a giant heap. In these circumstances, a ruined house was simply put to the torch while the soldiers gathered around to absorb as much warmth as possible.

The Russians were ever-present. Tanks were often just over the horizon. Occasionally, they would dash in for a blitz attack and then retreat as quickly as they came. The Russians expected that we could not survive this march, a reasonable conclusion in light of the trail of frozen corpses left behind the column. Why risk engaging the Germans if the cold could do the job with no casualties? None of us were about to disagree.

We knew that safety could only be found in the west. From our position at the firebase on the Don River to the safety of German lines would actually be less than 400 miles, as the crow flies. Without knowing our exact track, however, I would estimate that we traveled more than twice that distance over a period of about 12 weeks, heading to all points of the compass. Frigid wind and blizzards were frequent. Each time a winter storm fell upon us, we searched for shelter and waited it out as best we could. No one ever slept on the floor when we found shelter. The standard procedure was to fill the house or hut to the walls with soldiers. Jammed into the building like canned sardines, we slept shoulder-to-shoulder, standing on our frozen feet. As you can imagine, in this situation no one went outside to relieve himself during the night.

But the Russians kept us moving. Never content to engage us in a full battle, they would harass us with quick firefights, ambushes and night attacks. They were relentless. Each attack inflicted a wound somewhere along the *Rollbahn*, and, like a hemorrhaging sore, the life bled out of our column. Each time we emerged from our shelters after a storm or a night of frost and wind, there were fewer soldiers to continue.

One morning as I wedged against the window in a hut overlooking the *Rollbahn*, I saw a formation of Russian light tanks attack the column. They rolled in, shooting wildly and driving over the tops of sleds and vehicles, creating confusion, destroying equipment and crushing hapless soldiers who could not escape. Then they were gone, slipping heedlessly into the cold, gray fog.

The attacks continued, and casualties mounted. One day in early February I came upon a mechanized column of trucks and armored personnel carriers. Smoke rose from burnt-out vehicles. In some, truck drivers slumped over the wheel, no longer in pain. The battle could not have taken place more than an hour prior to my arrival. As I walked further through the wreckage, I found a bus with several beautiful women lying dead from bullet wounds. I believe they were entertainers who had been to the front during the holidays. The image of them haunts me to this day - so young and so attractive, but ravished by war and left to bleed on the frozen battlefield. There was nothing I could do; it was almost too much to comprehend.

As I walked through the line of destroyed vehicles, I discovered the means by which this column had been surprised. The Russians had built walls of snow far enough off the *Rollbahn* so they were difficult to see in the gray fog. As the column approached its closest point to this snow fort, the Russians opened up with withering machine-gun fire that was so devastating and accurate, no one in the column had a chance. Then they abandoned their guns and dashed back into the foggy mist.

I trudged on. For days and weeks... little changed, bitter cold winds, drifting snow, and everywhere death. I could feel lice all over my body. To this day I get chills remembering the awful feeling of being eaten alive. There was nothing I could do but keep moving and hope there would be enough of me left to rescue.

Two or three times we found large Wehrmacht storage warehouses filled to the roof with rations. Again we would load our pockets with everything we could carry. I emptied my gas mask canister and filled it with mayonnaise, a substance that was far more useful to my immediate needs. We passed through small Russian villages on almost a daily basis. As hungry as we were, none of those around me ever considered stealing a chicken or slaughtering a cow for food. We knew it could mean the death of an entire family. I resolved to die of starvation before I would ever take food from the mouth of a Russian.

Gradually, my feet and legs froze to the knee. Every step I took shot pain through my whole body and brought tears to my eyes. I prayed constantly to be delivered from this nightmare. I felt hopeless, but I refused to give up – one foot in front of the other.

* * * * * * *

By the end of February we had been trying to break out of the encirclement for almost eight weeks. The daily routine changed little. We marched; we stopped; we waited. We changed directions. If a skirmish erupted, we marched in a new direction. The wind blew bitter cold, and the snow drifted constantly. I had little feeling below my knees. The pain was unbearable.

One afternoon, I heard my name called as I passed through a deserted Russian village. I looked around and saw a soldier sitting in the doorway of a burned-out Russian house. I looked closer and finally recognized Harold from the 9th Battery. The change in his appearance shocked me, but I was overjoyed that I had found a comrade from my unit. I noticed there was a half- empty bottle of vodka between his knees. Sensing what was happening, I asked Harold to stop drinking.

"Come on Harold, walk along with me," I said.

"Where are you going?" he inquired nonchalantly.

I had no answer for him. I could see in his face that he had given up. There was nothing I could do to change his mind.

"I will empty this bottle, and when night comes I will fall asleep here, outside. When I wake up, I will find a better world."

I sat with him a moment, knowing I would never see him again. Death had a face, and it was my friend Harold. The inevitability of his fate stuck deeply into my heart. It was a pain I would come to know often in the coming years, but at this moment it seemed to overwhelm me. I knew I couldn't remain with him. I had to keep moving. With tears in my eyes I bade my friend farewell and turned westward again, never looking back, knowing that Harold was already gone.

* * * * * * *

During the weeks and months we meandered behind enemy lines, Russian Lieutenant General Golikov had pressed the Voronezh Front westward. On February 16, he drove the elite II SS Corps out of Kharkov. This rapid move forward drove a salient into the German Eastern Front, which created the empty, overrun territory through which we marched.[1] We were looking for a weak point in the Russian lines that we could break through to link up with Army Group Center under General Weichs.

Field Marshal Erich von Manstein was south of Army Group Center with his newly renamed Army Group Don. When General Golikov's troops occupied Kharkov, Manstein quickly saw the Russians were overextended.[2] On February 17, Field Marshal von Manstein had a meeting with Hitler in which he managed to persuade Hitler to allow him to counterattack into the Kharkov salient. If this could happen before the spring thaw, Manstein believed they could bring the Russian advance to a halt. Hitler consented. On February 19, the fleeing II SS Corps under General Hausser turned and counterattacked, catching the Russians completely by surprise. Supported by the Fourth Panzer Army and the Luftwaffe, together with Army Group Center and Army Group Don, the Germans pushed the Russians back and retook Kharkov on March 15.[3] The Russians suffered horrendous losses - more than 23,000 dead and many taken prisoner. The effect of this counteroffensive was to push the Russians back, closer to our beleaguered column.[4] Few, if any of us, had any idea what tactical moves were being made in front of us. But as the weeks moved on into March, the distant sound of battle grew nearer.

* * * * * * *

By the middle of March, bitterly cold winds and blowing snow still plagued our column. In an attempt to stop the spreading frostbite in my feet and legs, I found rags with which to wrap my boots and legs to try to restore warmth. I doubt that my efforts did any good, but I was nevertheless a sight to behold.

More German soldiers, together with Italians and Hungarians, had joined our group.[5] By now, the column was well defined and moving more as a unit. More importantly, we were moving steadily to the west. Our position was north of Kharkov, close to 400 miles northwest from our firebase on the Don Front. Yet as each day passed, soldiers grew weaker and wounds became infected and would not heal. It became impossible to care for seriously wounded and injured soldiers. Struggling through a blizzard and meeting a fellow soldier lying in the snow with his arms extended up to you, begging for help, was the worst possible situation I ever faced. As time wore on, it was happening constantly. With all of your heart and with all of your soul, you wanted to help these men. But if you stopped, the outcome was certain; you would die with them. Turning my back and leaving them behind was much more painful than struggling on my frozen feet. I began to worry the day might come when that pain would become unbearable, when I too would sit down with them, resigned to my fate.

One morning toward the end of March, many of the leaders in our column realized that it was impossible to carry on with the many wounded and disabled soldiers. They were dying in droves, and the conditions on the *Rollbahn* were contributing to their demise. The decision was made that if we continued dragging them on sleds, they would have no chance of survival. If they were left behind, there was a chance the Russians would provide medical assistance and help the wounded. Obviously, those who were able to move on would have a much better chance to survive.

I am certain that similar decisions have been faced many times throughout history, and I suspect the reality of the situation has always been the same. When our battery commander had shot himself the first night of our withdrawal, his last words had said it all: "Every man for himself!" It simply came down to the survival of the fittest. It was a hard, cold decision that lacked any semblance of kindness, compassion or charity. "We are leaving you behind because we can no longer help you." And that is precisely what happened. All the wounded, sick and injured soldiers were gathered in the center of a small Russian village, under the frozen bare branches of a few trees. The idea was that they could help themselves if they were clumped together, and that they would survive until the Russians arrived to help them. Yet we knew they would likely be machine-gunned. The Russians could not care for them any better than we could.

As we left them behind, their cries and pleas were the most gut-wrenching sounds I ever heard in the war; they haunt me to this day. If I had known any of them personally, I doubt that I could have walked away. But I was numb with pain and fatigue. I was tired, I was hungry, and I was losing hope. The realization was coming over me that it probably didn't matter anyway. If something dramatic didn't happen soon, we would all be dead.

Another morning as I hobbled along with the column, a soldier with a familiar face approached me. He asked me how far I expected to get hobbling along like a crippled rag-picker. I told him I had not stopped since I left my firebase on the Don Front, and I had no intent of stopping until I was safe behind German lines. He looked at me more closely and asked if I was from the 9th Battery. I answered affirmatively and then recognized that he was Hauptmann Fischer of the 11th Battery. He was in charge of a few sleds that still carried a few wounded soldiers, and he immediately found room for me on one of them. The pain I suffered from walking was over. Yet still I had to shelter myself from the cold. I covered myself with blankets and burrowed down under the straw. The icy wind continued to blow and the snow drifted over us, but I managed to find some protection. I soon found that while I had been walking, I had focused on the pain in my feet and legs. Now as I rode along on the sled, I noticed my hunger pains more than I had while walking. It seemed that when one pain resolved, there was another waiting to take its place.

For a few days in late March, there was a sudden break of spring weather. It was encouraging that we might be finished with this awful Russian winter. Then, as suddenly as spring came, it left again. Once more the bitterly cold winds howled and the snow continued to blind us. As I lay on the sled pondering my situation, I recalled my early thoughts when we began this march 12 weeks earlier. I had no idea of the hardship and pain that would be visited upon me for 12 weeks and, further, I could not believe that I had survived so far. Had I known what was ahead of me, I wondered if I could have made it. On the other hand, having survived 12 weeks of Hell, I was more resolved than ever to survive this march. I began to realize how I had been blessed and how my prayers had been answered. I began to see how all of this experience would give me strength and how I could truly fill the measure of my being. It was a refiner's fire for certain, however, without any flames. I thought perhaps a few of those refiners' flames might be helpful in my present situation but decided not to press my luck. I would accept my refiner's freeze.

* * * * * * *

Early one afternoon as the gray clouds hung low and the freezing wind continued to blow, we heard the drone of aircraft engines. These sounded familiar to me. Many feared that Russian planes were about to drop through the clouds and cut us to pieces. As it turned out, I was right. Three JU-52 aircraft dropped out of the clouds and landed within 100 meters of the *Rollbahn*. The pilots kept the engines running while crewmen opened the hatches. Several soldiers ran to the aircraft and jumped in. The pilots then took off into the gray sky. I thought that maybe I was dreaming, but as they turned and roared overhead, I knew it was real. Brave pilots were doing what little they could to help.

The column kept moving, sometimes fast, and other times very slowly. There were frequent stops, sometimes for hours. Then the column would pick up and move quickly. Our driver would coax our horse to get him to pull faster, but – alas – the poor horse looked worse than we did.

I noticed that a defensive line of soldiers had formed on both sides of the column. Beyond them were fog and the endless greyish-white, snow-filled plains with no recognizable features. I noticed these soldiers all carried their rifles in a ready position. I decided I would keep mine close at hand as well.

Rumors spread through the column constantly. We heard that German troops had broken through the Russian lines and there was an opening close ahead. The tension in the air could have been cut with a knife. Then we realized the rumors were true.

Suddenly, all around us were hundreds of lifeless olive- brown uniforms of the Red Army. As far as I could see, there were olive-brown patches on the frozen landscape. A battle had raged not long before our arrival, and soon we were passing foxholes where the familiar German uniforms of the elite II SS Korps were dug in protecting our escape. Behind them were lines of German tanks and artillery. Tears welled in my eyes as suddenly I felt an enormous release from tension and fear, replaced with joy and gratitude.

We had broken the Russian line just east of Sudzha, about 200 miles north-northwest of Kharkov. Units from the II SS Korps had succeeded in taking Belgorod, which was southeast of our position. The push had thinned the lines of the Russian 38th and 40th Armies, and we had broken through at the easternmost point of General Golikov's Voronezh Front. For the next few months, the Eastern Front would remain in roughly the same position it was in the day we broke through. This would end, however, with the furious battle for Kursk that would take place in the coming summer and would mark a major turning point in the collapse of the Eastern Front.

For me, however, the tactical situation was the last thing on my mind. German medical units moved us quickly into Russian huts whose floors had been covered with clean straw. Here I received my first hot meal in several weeks. Though it was still well below zero outside, the old Russian stove kept us warm. I received a new blanket; for the moment, it was a most prized possession. As I looked about the room, I counted about 50 soldiers, none of whom were familiar. I reflected on my ordeal, but it was impossible to grasp the enormity of this experience. My mind could only understand it as a nightmare from which I had just awakened. Yet the cries of anguish and the horrid condition of my fellow survivors confirmed that it was all very real. I closed my eyes and thanked God for sparing me, promising that someday I would find a way to show my gratitude.

I had survived, and hopefully I would see my home and my family again. I thought of my comrades who had not made it to safety; of Harold frozen in the snow, our captain buried where he fell, of lifeless, beautiful people ambushed in a surreal and horrible scene. I was lucky to survive but was also cursed with memories that would haunt me for the rest of my life.

Our medical teams next moved us into trucks that would take us to Sumy, where we boarded trains bound for Germany. The conditions were less than ideal, but at least we were headed home.

The air was filled with the rotten stench of decay and infection. There were cries of pain and calls for help. The pain in my feet and legs was so intense that I could no longer walk. The skin on my feet had fallen away, and there was horrible infection everywhere. The pain was terrible and excruciating, almost unbearable.

When we entered Germany, more efforts were made to clean us and provide first aid and treatment. The train continued on, the trip lasting several days.

When we arrived in Breslau, we were allowed off the train; however, we were not allowed to speak to any civilians. Most Germans knew about Stalingrad, and crowds of them gathered near the train station to see the ragged remnants of the German 6th Army. At Breslau, we received postcards to send home to let our families know that we were alive and heading to the hospital. Then it was back on the train. Finally, we arrived at an army hospital located at Witzenhausen, a small town east of Kassel in the state of Hesse, north of Frankfurt-on-Main.

As they carried me off the train, I looked about me and saw that it was spring. The trees on the hills were full of blossoms. The air was clean and mild. It was as if there were no such thing as war.

I was carried from the train and loaded into a Red Cross van. We drove through a sleepy town that was just awakening to a spectacularly beautiful morning. The hospital itself was new, situated in a meadow between two orchards of apple trees and cherry trees. Not far from the hospital buildings was a small, beautiful river, the Werra, which ran the length of this beautiful valley.

The fragrance was intoxicating as I waited my turn to enter the hospital. Lying on my stretcher in my lice-infested uniform, smelling like death and decay, I realized that I was now the flaw in an otherwise perfect setting. I closed my eyes and breathed in the fragrant aroma of spring. I could feel its immediate effect deep within my wounded body. My healing had begun. I was so happy to be at this hospital. I knew this would be the perfect place to recuperate. I had arrived in Heaven, having passed through the very depths of Hell.

CHAPTER 11
A TIME TO HEAL

WHEN I ARRIVED in my ward, a smiling, pleasant nurse, who held a huge pair of scissors in her hands, greeted me. With a few skillful snips, she peeled me out of my smelly uniform; another snip or two and I found myself out of my underwear. It had happened so quickly that I had little opportunity to protest in the name of modesty. A brief survey of the room revealed that I was not the only man lying in my birthday suit in front of all those attractive nurses. Thinking back, I believe this was the first time I had ever found myself in such a position, at least since the day I was born!

It was impossible for me to shower, so two nurses set about scrubbing my filthy body from head to toe. I closed my eyes and gritted my teeth. I soon discovered that these were dedicated nurses who were professionals that understood the circumstances. But it, nevertheless, did little for my dignity. They were sensitive to my embarrassment. Soon I was comfortable, knowing that I was being cared for with respect and empathy.

The nurses dressed me in pajamas and put me into bed. Again I looked about the room searching in vain for a familiar face. What had become of the 9th Battery? We had scattered to the four winds on the icy steppes of Russia. Was I the only survivor of my unit?

Heavy doses of pain medication and soft music soon lulled me into a deep, restful sleep, the best I had known in a long time. When I awakened later in the afternoon, a group of doctors and nurses were making the rounds to each patient, speaking softly to each of them. Then it was my turn. They asked questions about my unit, where and how I had received my injuries and other questions about my experiences. Then they looked at my feet. I saw eyebrows go up and heard soft murmurings that I could not completely make out. But I did hear the unsettling word "amputation." They then spoke directly to me, giving me words of encouragement before moving on to the next patient.

Later a nurse brought special equipment to my bed that resembled an arch roughly 30 inches high and about three feet wide. It was made of wood and had special lights inside. "Let's try this first," she said, as she placed it over my feet. Over the next few days and weeks, the radiant heat from these lights gradually stopped the infectious discharge from my feet. Ever so slowly, they began to heal.

* * * * * * *

Each night at 10 o'clock, a nurse would enter and say good night to all of us. Then the lights would go out and I would be alone with my thoughts. Each night my mind would wander back to the frozen Russian steppes, to the bitterly cold wind and blowing snow. I would see our Battery Chief slowly put the pistol to his head and end his life. I would relive my conversation with Harold over and over again, wondering what I might have said or done to convince him to move on. I could hear the voices of thousands of soldiers begging me to help them. I could see the hopeless condition of wounded soldiers I could not help. They haunted me every night. More than once I would awake in the middle of the night with the sickening sensation that lice were once again crawling over my body, eating me alive. These haunting memories remain with me to this very day.

Other times at night I would awaken to the deep, thunderous roar of the RAF on their night bombing runs, looking for targets in larger cities, perhaps south toward Frankfurt. At first, the Allies were idealistic in their early war claims that they would use precision bombing to take out military targets in Germany. It was almost impossible for them to pinpoint their targets without also hitting civilians. In the horrific fire-bombing of Hamburg in July 1943, the Allies used high explosives and incendiary bombs that killed almost 45,000 German civilians. The strategic aims of the allies officially changed to a policy of "carpet bombing" to ensure that strategic targets were destroyed. From our viewpoint, however, this change simply brought the policy more in line with the results.[1] And this strategy would kill hundreds of thousands of German civilians throughout the remainder of the war. The use of high explosives and incendiaries in these man-made firestorms literally sucked the oxygen out of the lungs of terrified civilians as they hid in shelters. The heat of the inferno actually melted pots and pans as well as the asphalt in the streets.

The Germans who died in these air raids were just as innocent as the 60,000 Britons who died in Hitler's murderous blitzes and rocket attacks. In war, hate begets hate; I had seen this first hand on the Eastern Front. The insanity of extremism had started this conflict, and nothing could stop it. Unfortunately, all sides became caught up in revenge and hatred. When the war ended, tens of millions of soldiers and civilians had died; in Russia alone, more than twenty million. War was, indeed, Hell.

* * * * * * *

One morning a pretty nurse arrived at my bedside and asked if I would like to go for a walk. I wasn't so sure I could do this, but the invitation was too good to pass up. Holding her arm, I began to stroll up and down the corridors. Even though it felt like I was walking on broken glass, I assured her the pleasure of her company was worth the discomfort. Each day we would walk a little farther, and each day it became less and less painful.

Other patients in my ward were being discharged. As soon as one bed opened, there was a new patient from the front. Mostly these soldiers suffered from bullet and shrapnel wounds. I continued to take longer and longer walks, and soon the doctors came to watch my progress. They were very pleased. It appeared that, before long, I would be released from the hospital.

arent's Wedding Day - April 1920. Uncle Max Is directly behind the bride-
room, Arthur Oscar Naujoks, Sr. Mother-in-law is next to the bride, Ida
oeper Naujoks.

Tilsit Primary - 1931. Art is in the front, the fourth from the left. Below, New Year's Eve - 1935. Art is on the front row, next to the accordion player.

New Year's Eve - 1937. Art is in the center back row with his friend's arm around him. Note the Pathfinder uniforms. Below, Rositten - summer of 1939, the last days before the war. Art is on the right.

At the organ - 1939. Below, President Shultzke's home - 1939. Note the various uniforms and ranks.

Art's eighteenth birthday - Christmas 1940. His friends are starting to appear in uniform. Below, Art and friends on an outing after church - 1941. Art is second from left.

*Art is inducted in the German Army in late August 1941. He is
immediately appointed OFA or "Officer Anwärter."*

Art in France during the spring of 1942. Below Art is relaxed on sentry duty. (Picture is blurred on original).

On train to Stalingrad, summer 1942. Art is in upper left-hand corner. Harold is sitting to the right next to Rockel standing. Eight months later Art is the only survivor.

9th Battery caisson just after emerging from the forest onto the steppes in the Ukraine - summer 1942.

...omel - summer 1942. The 9th Battery has just left the train and is taking to its ...eels and wheels." Note the horse-drawn caissons.

9th Battery on the Don Front - late summer 1942. Art is on the far right. Art is th only survivor of the 9th Battery. Below, the Don Bend can be seen in the background.

ᵗʰ Battery taking aim. Below, Art is awarded the Iron Cross, 2ⁿᵈ Class for t retreating during a surprise Soviet offensive in late September 1942. is the last time a senior officer survives him to award a medal. (Picture blurred).

Relaxing with friends after church - November 1942. Below, Sister Waltraut before church, sometime near November 19, 1942.

aking the most of leave - November 1942. Art with date seeing the sites in nd around Tilsit.

Recuperating in Tilsit, summer 1943.

Art as instructor at Heilsburg, East Prussia during 1943-44. This is the last surviving photograph of Art through the end of the war.

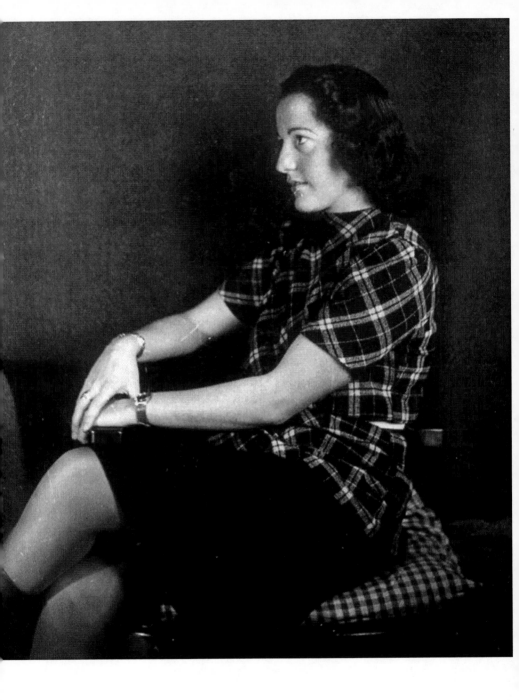

tta just before Art's last farewell, February 18, 1945.

East German missionaries - 1946-47. Art is in the back-center. Below, Art and companion take a bit of relaxation.

A passer-by stops to look at a handbill for the Leipzig conference.
Below, the Leipzig conference.

Wedding Day - October 25, 1947.

Home in Chemnitz - 1948.

Below. Radio Free Europe staff in Berlin - 1950. Art is on the far left.

Art, Traudy, and little sister Elly in Berlin - 1951.

As spring turned to summer, my wounds were healing nicely. With the aid of a cane, I could move around the hospital fairly well. For me, it was a miracle that I was walking again, and I couldn't get enough of the warm sunshine and fresh air. I was eager to get home and see my family again. They now knew I was in the hospital, but in March they had received a terrible shock when the Wehrmacht told them I was missing in action. A few weeks later, they received my postcard from Breslau and shortly after my arrival at the hospital were again notified that I was alive and recuperating in Witzenhausen.

I was finally released and sent home for a month of vacation. My arrival was a somber one, tears both of joy and of gratitude. We all held one another tight, so very grateful to be together again. The effect Stalingrad had on me was evident in my limp and walking cane. My family also saw deep spiritual wounds which would take time to heal. They saw the sadness in my eyes and steeliness in my composure that still held a lot inside. I was not the jovial soldier home on leave they had seen last November. There were no tales of adventure to share with my family, only nightmares that needed to be quietly let go.

I spent many hours sitting in the garden, surrounded by lovely flowers, birds and bees, drawing beauty from nature that could heal the emotional scars of war. These solitary hours were crucial to restoring my soul, taking the time to appreciate things in the world I had always taken for granted. It helped me come to grips with my past - to face it and deal with the frozen ghosts on the barren steppes of Russia. The peace and tranquility of home helped me to balance myself again and to prepare for an uncertain future.

* * * * * * *

At the end of my four weeks at home, I received orders to report to my reserve training camp. It had moved from Insterburg to Heilsburg, a small town in East Prussia. I was pleased to discover the camp was entirely new, from the comfortable three-story buildings with wide windows, to the training grounds and new swimming pool. I was still recovering and was not fit for combat, So the question remained: What was I good for?

One morning the Camp Commander called me to his office for an interview. A major, he had many questions as he went through my files, probing my experience to find my strengths that could be useful to his command. Finally, he decided that I could best serve the war effort by training recruits rather than waiting for my recovery to be complete so I could return to the front. The war was creating heavy demand for more reservists, and training for recruits had been put on an accelerated schedule. He assigned me to the communications battery to train recruits in the use of communications equipment, something in which I had extensive experience.

I was assigned my own quarters, with a recruit to be responsible for keeping my room in good order. Now this was the life! The classrooms were roomy and well equipped, my quarters were comfortable, and I had a seemingly endless supply of students. The assignment would be for one year, during which time I would have the opportunity to see many recruits coming and going. The assignment was challenging and one that I knew would be rewarding. Excused from outside activities, I exercised and continued my rehabilitation on my own. In short, it was a dream assignment.

* * * * * *

One day not long after my arrival at camp, a new member was assigned to our staff. His last name was Karcher. He was a mystery to most of us as he had no rank insignia. None of our superiors gave us any explanation regarding this fellow, but it was obvious that even the Camp Commander treated him with kid gloves. He was perhaps ten years older than I, a handsome fellow with an air of mystery about him. He talked often about his hometown of Vienna and showed me pictures of his wife and children. Whenever the conversation turned toward politics or the war, he was very fanatical in his support of and admiration for Adolf Hitler. I knew I had to be careful in what I said to him.

I had never been a fan of Hitler or the NSDAP. After Stalingrad, I doubted he was capable of effective military leadership at any level. Some of the survivors knew of his order to defend Stalingrad to the last man and his refusal to allow for withdrawals when it was tactically expedient. "Surrender out of the question . . . " Hitler stated in a message to the Sixth Army.[2]   Many Germans died because of his fanaticism. General Paulus had asked for permission to withdraw from Stalingrad when it became hopeless. His request was denied. Then Hitler made him a field marshal. No German field marshal had ever surrendered, and Hitler expected that Paulus would not allow himself to be the first. Rather than put a pistol to his head, Field Marshal Paulus defied Hitler's order and surrendered, stating, "I have no intention of shooting myself for this Bohemian corporal."[3]

Field Marshal von Manstein had stood up to Hitler. He saw the tactical advantage at Kharkov after the fall of Stalingrad and demanded that Hitler allow a counterattack. For his courage, I owed him my life.

* * * * * * *

As my acquaintance with Herr Karcher became more casual, he began to share more about his life. One afternoon as we walked out of the main gate, I noticed the guards saluted him as he passed; yet he still had no rank insignia! When I asked him about this, he said, "Come, I will show you something." I visited with him in his quarters, where he showed me a curious red linen book emblazoned with a gold swastika. I had never seen a book like this before. It listed the names of individuals who were members of the *Blutorden* or Blood Order. As I came to find out, the *Blutorden* had been organized by the Nazi Party in 1934, at first to honor those who had participated with Hitler in the Beer Hall Putsch of November 9, 1923, in Munich. Since 1934, more members had been admitted to the *Blutorden* for extreme loyalty and sacrifice to the Nazi Party. I believe Herr Karcher of Vienna was one of these newer members. He told me he had been arrested several times, and had even been shot by the police. He was a Nazi activist who helped establish the NSDAP in Austria. He had shed his blood for the party, and his reward was admission to the *Blutorden*.

There were several pages that described his background as well as a picture of him in his Nazi uniform. I had never heard of the *Blutorden*, and I suspected there were not many Germans who knew of this somewhat secret society. It was obvious that Herr Karcher was very proud of his membership in this order, and that his loyalty to the Nazi Party was the driving force of his life. I had never met anyone who hated Jews as much as Herr Karcher. It was unnerving to me to hear his interpretation of world history in light of his anti-Semitism. As a Mormon, I had a profoundly different view of Jews, believing that they were still God's chosen people. Clearly, however, this was not a topic of conversation for Herr Karcher, and I was not motivated in the slightest to bring up my own religious beliefs. The Nazis considered Mormons to be dangerous and counter to their ideals.

I decided it was prudent that I not become a close friend of Herr Karcher for the obvious reason of our polar opposite view on politics and religion. I now understood why all members of the camp administration showed him so much deference. It was curious to me, however, as to why he was here as a soldier in the Wehrmacht. Was he being punished for some misdeed? More likely, I thought, he was here to observe and to ensure that all of our recruits were not only properly trained but also properly indoctrinated at the same time. For whatever reason, he never explained his situation to me.

Because my family had already had its brush with the Nazis some years before when Uncle Max had been captured as an anti- Nazi and eventually executed, I was naturally intimidated by anyone deeply involved in the Nazi Party. I didn't want anyone knocking on my mother's door asking if she wanted to pay for my burial. So I had to be careful in how I distanced myself from Herr Karcher. It could not be so obvious that he might become suspicious that I had something to hide. There is no doubt that he reviewed my service records, which in my case showed that I had survived the Battle of Stalingrad. I had been awarded the Iron Cross Second Class after the memorable tank battle in September 1942, and I was a loyal German soldier. But, alas, I was not a member of the Nazi Party. For the entire year that I remained at the Recruit Training Center, I was never questioned or bothered. But my fears were not unlike the fears of most Germans who wondered if there would ever come a knock in the night.

My assignment at the training camp went by quickly. I gradually regained my strength and, before too long, was able to put away my walking cane. I continued to enjoy lecturing and training recruits in communications, making many acquaintances among the recruits.

In the summer of 1944, my assignment as an instructor was over. I gathered my combat gear and was soon reassigned to the Eastern Front. When I had departed Russia in April 1943, I had to travel about 1,000 miles to return to Germany. Now, in the summer of 1944, the Russians had made my trip shorter; it was only about 300 miles back to the front.

CHAPTER 12

BACK TO THE FRONT

BY THE EARLY summer of 1944, the Russians had recovered over half of the territory lost to the Germans since June 1941. Though Germany had lost ground to the Russians in the previous 18 months, the Russians still did not have decisive control on the Eastern Front. However, the overwhelming number of soldiers sent into the field by the Red Army soon outnumbered the 2.2 million German soldiers protecting a weak line of defense stretching from East Prussia to the Black Sea.

The Normandy invasion of June 6 required an enormous commitment of German troops and equipment to fight the Allies in the west, who would soon be much closer to Germany than the Russians. Stalin finally had the second front he had been waiting for and quickly moved to increase his strategic advantage. He knew the Germans could not effectively reinforce their eastern defenses and that his offensive strikes would eventually be unstoppable. Further, the effect of round-the-clock allied bombing of Germany's war factories had also taken its toll on Germany's capacity to fight. It was obvious that things were about to get worse for the Wehrmacht.

On the Ukrainian Front, the massive Red Army continued to press westward and, in March, nearly destroyed the First Panzer Army in an encirclement around Kamenets Podolsky, near the Dniester River in

Western Ukraine. Field Marshal von Manstein flew to Obersalzburg for another confrontation with Hitler, this time over reinforcements. He succeeded in moving the II Panzer Korps from France to the Ukraine, but eventually lost his command. At the beginning of April, the command was renamed Army Group North Ukraine, and von Manstein was relieved by Field Marshal Walther Model.[1]

In June, Model would also take command of Army Group Center. Actually, he took command of the gap where Army Group Center had once been. It was just after Germany suffered its greatest, most disastrous loss on the Eastern Front - 25 divisions destroyed in Belorussia. By July 5, 1944, the Fourth Army had lost 130,000 of its 165,000 troops, First Panzer Army had lost a similar number, and the Ninth Army had collapsed. In all, more than 350,000 German soldiers were lost in a disaster far worse than Stalingrad.[2] On July 17, around 57,000 German prisoners captured in Belorussia were paraded through Moscow in front of a quiet crowd of Russians. It seemed as if everyone was sick of this war, the political struggle between two despots in the east. Some of the older Russian women wept for these young men who would likely never see home again.[3]

The Russian soldiers in Belorussia, however, had no sympathy for German soldiers. The Red Army continued to find mass grave after mass grave of murdered Russian Jews and partisans behind the German retreat. The efforts of Hitler's elite SS troops to ensure racial purity, even in retreat, showed nothing to the world except hatred and bigotry.

To be sure, German soldiers who had nothing to do with Nazi politics and beliefs suffered greatly for the atrocities of the SS and Gestapo.[4]

It was into this caldron of fire and brimstone that I arrived in the summer of 1944 to try to defend my homeland from a very angry enemy.

* * * * * *

I reported to a unit on the Army Group North Ukraine front line about 60 miles east of Lemberg, or Lvov as it is known today. To my surprise, the members of this unit were all Austrian. I was very happy to be among Austrians because of their relaxed and casual manner, their beautiful clean dialect of German, and their not-so-military way of doing things. Introduced to the Battery Commander, I learned this unit was, indeed, one of Hitler's favorites. I should feel just as much at home here as I would in a Prussian outfit. This, I assured him, I would do. My image of these elite Austrian pets of Hitler, however, was about to change.

Early one morning in mid-July 1944, I was up early, about 5:00 a.m., writing letters on my day off. Suddenly, the air was filled with tremendous explosions, and the earth began to quake violently.[5] I had never experienced such a barrage. The Russians had commenced a tremendous fusillade of heavy artillery, and shells were bursting above and all around me. Dirt and smoke filled the air, and shrapnel whistled all around with lethal randomness. The explosions were deafening and deadly as they found their mark in the various trenches and emplacements around us. It was impossible to walk or even speak or hear commands without screaming, and there was a lot of screaming going on.

As I looked around, I saw all of these elite Austrian troops frozen in their tracks. No one moved. They were panic-stricken. These weren't soldiers! They couldn't hold a candle to my dead comrades from the 9th Battery. Where was our leadership? It disgusted me.

The heaviest barrage targeted our left flank. We watched as the Russians broke through in a hailstorm of artillery shells followed by fast-moving tanks and infantry. Artillery explosions pocked the landscape with craters. Tangled barbed wire, smashed timbers and chunks of concrete were everywhere. While it appeared there were many obstacles to slow a tank assault, there was also a lot of cover for the advancing Red Army troops.

Suddenly, all communications to our command bunker were gone. A telephone cable had been hit and we had to repair it. Which of these brave soldiers of Hitler's favorite unit would repair it? This problem was not my responsibility, but it was obvious we were all sitting ducks if we did not repair the phone line, and repair it quickly. As I looked around, there was still no direction or leadership coming from the senior officers. Their panic was deadly, and I now understood why no decision was worse than a bad decision. I grabbed my steel helmet and yelled above the roar.

"Any of you have the guts to go with me?"

A young private forced his way forward and said, "I'll go!"

"Good! Grab that cable and let's go."

As we ran out of the bunker, the crescendo of exploding artillery shells grew louder and more frequent. The bursts were close and deafening. We were constantly looking for cover, digging in as deep as we could each time we heard the whistle of an incoming shell. The Russians were targeting every square inch of our position, and the explosions were endless. We scrambled from crater, to trench, to foxhole, kissing the dirt again and again in a macabre dance of life and death. Soon we found the break in the line and set about repairing it while artillery rounds burst all around us. On one occasion I ducked late and an explosion went off right in front of me. My ears were ringing, but as I lay there for a moment it seemed like I was OK. I turned to see if my companion was still with me. He was fine except for the look of fear on his face.

"Sir! Your face is covered with blood!"

We finished the repair, and tried to find a route away from the withering fire. We stumbled through deserted trenches and across more battlefield debris until we finally found a bunker where some German soldiers administered first aid to the shrapnel wound on my forehead. I told my companion that he should not try to return to our battery, but that he should help me find the division command center. He seemed very relieved.

As we rested for a moment, I was amazed at the ferocity of this artillery fire. It had not let up in the slightest and actually seemed to be growing more intense. My companion was very nervous, but I admired his bravery. I tried to calm him down and get his mind off this horrific bombardment.

"Where are you from, private?"

"Dusseldorf, sir, I am from Dusseldorf."

"Ahh, so you are another lousy Prussian like me!"

He grinned.

Moments later we were again on the run, this time in search of our division command center. Once we found it, I was sent to a nearby field hospital where my head wound could be properly treated. I went from hospital to hospital over the next few days for treatment of this shrapnel wound. Finally, after about a week or so, I was released to return to the front. By this time, however, there was nothing left of the Austrian division. Twelve thousand men were either dead or marching eastward to Siberia.

In August I was sent to a camp near the city of Oppeln, where I would become a part of a newly formed division made up mostly of East Prussian soldiers assembled to defend our homeland. Oppeln was the old capital of Upper Silesia and an important rail junction about 50 miles southeast of Breslau. It was a beautiful setting, right on the Oder River in the midst of rolling hills, dark forests and open meadows. Here I would recuperate for a short time from my wounds while the Wehrmacht assembled the new division.

Nearby our camp was a POW compound occupied by American, British and Canadian officers. Only an eight-foot chain-link fence surrounded the camp, and security seemed minimal. I had a lot of spare time, so I decided to walk this fence line and have a good look at my "enemies." I saw that these prisoners would form up early each morning and report to the commandant of the camp. These Allied officers seemed relaxed and cordial. Often during this morning report there would be laughter among the ranks as if they were enjoying some humorous moments.

Some of these officers were cultivating small gardens along the fence, which to me appeared to be tended with a great deal of care and pride. I walked the fence many times, but never had the opportunity to speak with any of them. I didn't think I could consider any of these men my enemy. They were gentlemen doing their duty in this crazy war. About the only fault I ever found with these POWs was the horrible sound of bagpipes that awakened us each morning. This fellow from Scotland was truly doing his level best to carry on the war while a POW, and it was working very effectively.

New soldiers arrived at Oppeln daily. By the end of August we moved out to our new position on the front lines. We dug in north of Warsaw, opposite the oncoming juggernaut of Marshal Rokossovsky's ferocious First Belorussian Front, which had wiped out the German armies near Minsk. It was said that all the Russian military commanders were very competitive, and each wanted to be the first to Berlin. Their competitiveness translated into very aggressive and bold tactical moves that had been effective in driving the Germans back into Poland. Now, however, our homeland was at risk, and I wondered if this would strengthen the resolve of my comrades. Only time would tell.

* * * * * * *

Our battery took a position overlooking the Narrew River about 15 miles north of Warsaw. As we approached our position, we came upon a low hill that stood out like a sore thumb in this very flat countryside. It was covered with bushes and trees. At the base there was a mysterious entrance. Going inside, we found an open square surrounded by 15-foot walls covered in vines and grass. This was a casemate that had been built in the 18th or 19th century for the defense of Warsaw. It connected to Warsaw and several other casemates around the city through old tunnels roughly 10 feet high and 10 feet wide.

The casemate had several rooms, all of which were crumbling and run down despite the walls and ceiling being 8 feet thick, maybe even more. It was very comfortable inside this old fortification, knowing that Russian artillery would probably be unable to penetrate it. Even so, everyone had a nagging feeling that, as safe as it appeared to be, it still seemed we were sitting in a mousetrap.

Nevertheless, we went to work, digging trenches and setting up our equipment. Our trenches were only about five feet deep; at that point we reached the top of the casemate. But the view was incredible. I had the best observation point I had ever had in this war. I could see directly into the Russian trenches and had a clear view for miles and miles. The unfortunate side to this seeming advantage was that the Russians could see our casemate too.

After we set up communications with the battery, I began targeting several Russian emplacements. The fire from our 150mm Howitzer was very effective, and in a short period of time we had taken out several Russian positions. My success dwindled, however, as my position was soon identified and targeted by the Russians. I had more than I had bargained for, and soon Russian artillery shells began raining down on our position. I didn't want to test the strength of the walls and ceiling of this casemate, so we decided it was a good time to fall back to another position. Several miles later we found a more suitable position that was safer and operationally effective, but without the lovely view the casemate had provided.

* * * * * * *

Our position north of Warsaw remained stable for the next several weeks. It was fall, and soon the leaves would be gone and winter would be upon us. It was certainly not like the steppes of Russia, but it would still be cold and miserable. It was much more difficult to spot targets in this landscape of flat fields and small farmhouses between patches of forest. My best positions seemed to be the attics of some of these farmhouses.

One day in early October, I heard a breathtaking roar to the south of us. I looked up and saw the sky filled with four-engine bombers heading over Warsaw. None of us had ever seen anything like this. Was this the new *Wunder-Waffe* that Hitler had been promising, the new super weapon of the Luftwaffe that would turn the tide of the war? We quickly called the command post, and as we watched the quizzical expression on the phone talker's face, we soon learned the terrible truth.

Bursts of German antiaircraft fire began blossoming in black mourning-cloth puffs over Warsaw. The roar came from American bombers that had flown all the way from England to drop supplies and support the Warsaw uprising. Suddenly, thousands of parachutes bloomed in the midst of the anti-aircraft fire, carrying canisters of supplies to the Polish insurgents trapped in Warsaw and hoping for a miracle. This drop, however, would not answer their prayers. The parachutes drifted wide, and most all the supplies fell into German hands, a welcome boost for the oncoming fight with the Russians.

On October 2, the uprising collapsed and the Polish partisans surrendered to the SS troops, who took quick and brutal revenge against the hapless resistance fighters who had held out so long for Russian relief. Alas, the Russians were suffering from the same strained lines of supply that had plagued the Wehrmacht for so long. For lack of fuel and ammunition, the Russian drive to the west had ground to a halt, leaving the uprising to certain failure. When fuel and ammunition did catch up, it was too late for these partisans, many of whom were tortured and executed.

Early one afternoon in early October I was moving with my group to a forward observation position at the front line, when a big dust cloud appeared moving toward us from the rear. We moved off the road and turned to watch as an armored troop carrier with several high ranking officers roared by. Suddenly it squealed to a halt and an officer jumped off the vehicle calling my name. I was stunned; it was von Langenstein from my old 9th Battery, now a colonel (*Oberst*) with a big grin on his face. He gave me a big bear hug and lifted me off my feet laughing. We looked at each other in total disbelief, expressing more emotion with our eyes than we had time to speak. "I hope I see you again soon!" he said, as he dashed back to the carrier. I waved as he drove off, and I never saw him again.

* * * * * *

During the weeks since our East Prussian Division had been formed, I had the opportunity to look around and get a feeling for the soldiers who were fighting next to me. Youth and age seemed to be the most common factors that were readily identifiable. The young soldiers had no experience and had never been to the front. Their training was marginal and I doubted they would last in the type of intense combat we had seen earlier that summer. The older soldiers were perhaps better trained, but they too lacked front-line combat experience. All of them had come to the front to defend East Prussia. By October, I began to have serious doubts.[6]

From my observation posts in the attics of farmhouses and hanging from the limbs of tall trees, I watched the buildup that was developing on the Russian side of the front. It occurred to me the Russians could easily turn toward the Baltic. If they did so, East Prussia would be surrounded.

I decided it was time to warn Mother. I wrote her a letter and advised her that if there were any way for her to leave East Prussia, now would be a good time. Our household goods had been reduced substantially because of a few bomb attacks. It would not be difficult for her to pack what was left and move to a safer location in Germany. My fear for my family's safety grew daily, and I prayed fervently that they would get out in time.

The problem we could not solve, however, was the fact that my father had been ordered to remain behind and dig trenches for the defense of Tilsit. As you can imagine, the parting of my parents was heartbreaking. My mother would later describe to me how each of them stared deeply into each other's eyes, trying to soak up as much love and memories as they possibly could before parting. It was a parting that both of them believed would certainly be their last. War had caused them immeasurable grief and fear, and it took every ounce of faith they could muster to let go of that embrace. My father would have nothing to do with the idea of Grandmother, Mother and my younger sister staying behind for his sake. It gave him great peace of mind and courage to know that they would be safe.

Some time later, I received a letter from my mother postmarked from a small village near Freiburg in Saxony. For the time being, they were safe; but my father, like me, was on his own.

CHAPTER 13

HOUSE OF CARDS

WINTER HAD ARRIVED in Poland. It was not the biting cold of the Russian steppes that would freeze-dry exposed flesh in a matter of minutes. But it was still freezing cold and miserable to endure. The mud from the fall rains was freezing into a hard surface perfect for Russian tank assaults. It didn't take a genius to figure out that everything was about to change. The winter freeze, with the gradual buildup of Russian forces we had been watching for the last several weeks, all added up to the conclusion that a new winter offensive was soon coming to our neighborhood.

During the lull in fighting through October and November, I perfected the art of forward observation by trying several different strategies. As the leaves fell, trees became useless. Sitting in open branches with no leaves for cover, you were a duck in a shooting gallery. I couldn't help but notice these bare trees standing out in the snowscape, their dark trunks and branches raised in surrender. Was it an omen?

As fall hardened into winter, my most effective observation post was in the attic of a Polish farmhouse. I would cut a small hole in the roof through which I could poke my range finder periscopes. On a good day, I could see about five or six miles; but as the season wore on, my vision became impaired by the overcast skies, rain, fog, blowing snow, and combinations of these.

The Russian infantry had become wise to the tactics of the German Wehrmacht, especially when it came to artillery bombardment of their positions. Seasoned Russian soldiers became adept at searching for the obvious locations where a German forward artillery observer, such as me, might hide and call heavy artillery shells down on Russian positions. Anticipating this, I always built a small redoubt within these Polish farmhouse attics with bricks, rocks, heavy timbers and anything else that would protect me from Russian bullets. It didn't take long after I had made my first calls for fire before the Russians located my position and brought on heavy fire from small arms. When they got close enough to use mortars, it was time for me to leave. Another terror was the possibility of Russian snipers waiting for us as we fell back. These snipers were deadly accurate and had made a name for themselves in Stalingrad, where they had methodically assassinated high-ranking German officers. I was a highly skilled observer, and thus a target important to them.

Once in a while, the weather cleared and we could see many targets of opportunity. Much to my frustration, however, the call for fire had recently added a new procedure. A staff officer at regimental headquarters who would evaluate each target that we called in was now controlling the tactical bombardment of Russian positions. He would scratch his chin and ask stupid questions.

"Is the target moving?"

"No, Hauptmann, it drove away a long time ago!"

"Then you have no target, correct?"

"That is correct, sir."

"Then permission to fire is denied!"

It was frustrating to watch Russian targets come into my range finder, only to escape because of the target evaluator's failure to respond quickly. On other occasions he approved the firing order but limited the number of rounds to around 12, sometimes not enough to destroy the target effectively. The target then escaped to fight another day, to kill my comrades in arms and maybe kill me.

The facts were simple. Germany was running out of ammunition and fuel, two of the most critical elements required when fighting a war. Allied bombing had destroyed our munitions factories, our refineries, and our ballbearing factories. Thousands of Allied fliers had lost their lives in the deadly raids over Germany, and they had not died in vain for their cause. In the last weeks of fall, we soldiers on the Eastern Front were feeling the brunt of the Allies' strategic air strikes. As more and more targets slipped from the view of my range finder, due to waiting for the approval of an ill-trained officer several miles to the rear, I soon realized that perhaps my most effective method of observation was simply to close my eyes.

* * * * * * *

Christmas 1944 came and went – not so hopeless as the Christmas I had spent two years earlier on the Don Front, but still depressing. Then, I had expected that Christmas of 1942 would be my last. Now two more had come and gone, and I considered both of them to be great blessings. What would Christmas 1945 bring? Would I live so long? Maybe I would be living under the rule of Godless communists who would ban the observance altogether. The only thing that seemed certain was that we were defending a wide front in a very precarious situation. Our troops were mostly inexperienced old men and boys. Our fuel was low. We were running out of ammunition. But, as I thought to myself, we weren't surrounded . . . yet!

* * * * * * *

The Russians were never ones to disappoint, and on January 12, 1945, the long-awaited Russian offensive began. The largest offensive of the war, more than 2.5 million Russian troops burst through German lines at 12 different locations. This massive Red Army was backed by enormous artillery firepower and an overwhelming superiority in tanks, all of which drew on a limitless supply of fuel and ammunition. It was a juggernaut that blew through our house of cards in a single puff.

The attack was not so intense in our sector, but on both flanks the Russians had blown past us. Unless we withdrew, there was a danger that our division would be encircled. On our left flank, elements of Marshal Rokossovsky's Second Belorussian Front moved northwest toward Danzig in a move to split Army Group Center, trapping its northern flank against the Baltic Sea.[1] This was the move I had feared would happen three months earlier. I was so grateful that my mother, sister and grandmother were now safe in Freiberg. My father, however, was in harm's way, and I feared for his safety constantly.

On our right flank, Marshal Zhukov, now in command of the First Belorussian Front, drove past us to the west, pushing for the Oder River. There he would be poised to strike at Berlin, less than 50 miles away. German resistance was game, but no match for the overpowering numbers streaming from the east. All we could do was fight with what we had and hope that we would not be killed or captured.

* * * * * * *

One morning shortly after the offensive began, it was again my turn to rotate to the forward observation post. Communications had been confusing, and there was not much information about our own infantry positions. It was a very cold day. A dense fog had descended over the frozen landscape, dropping visibility to about twenty feet. I was not comfortable with the situation. It was obvious my skills would not provide much help today.

A driver met me at the *Feuerstellung*, insisting that I go with him to the forward positions so he could deliver supplies. He had no idea where the front lines were, and in this fog he would surely become lost. So we followed his wagon onto the frozen road that led eastward to our position. The ruts were frozen, which caused the wheels of the wagon to make a terrible racket as they rolled over the uneven surface. As we passed through a Polish village, a sudden orange flash and bang sent shrapnel whistling over my head and into the side of a nearby house. Another explosion hit a wall nearby, and we dove for cover. I yelled at the driver to turn his wagon around and find his way back.

We quickly moved away from the road and disappeared between the houses to find cover. I crept around back toward the road where I could just barely make out the shadow of a Russian tank sitting in the middle of the road, directly in front of the path we had been following. The fog had made it almost impossible to see anything. Had the Russians waited only a few minutes more, we would all have been dead.

The tank kept firing a few more rounds, but he was just as blind as we were. Then it was quiet. I waited to see if he would start his engines and move up the road, but nothing happened. Quietly, I moved back to my men, and we silently moved out of the village, away from the tank. Not far outside the village, we found our forward trenches.

Night had fallen, and it was impossible to see anything besides a hazy blackness that strangled you with a blanket of hoarfrost. It burned your lungs to breathe it in, but the fear that gripped your soul only allowed short gasps. I could hear my heart pounding through my chest as I realized there were no soldiers in these trenches!

Hadn't I seen this before? As we quietly tried to find our way around in this labyrinth, it was impossible to make out anything. There were no sentries to challenge us; there were no soldiers to give us directions. I was reliving a nightmare! Finally, we found our bunker, but it was empty. The previous team had returned to the *Feuerstellung* before we could relieve it. I ordered my men to set up the equipment and contact the *Feuerstellung*. Once we had made contact, an excited voice repeated the same order over and over.

"Return at once, return at once!"

I could not believe it! I was so angry I could barely control myself. What kind of idiot would order us to this forward position without knowing the tactical situation first! It was beyond understanding. We quickly packed our gear, then slowly and quietly moved out of the bunker. The fog was there to greet us with its frozen, suffocating vapors as we made our way through the blackness. My mind was racing as I considered the mistakes that had been made to land me right where I swore I would never be again. I fought to keep my cool, knowing that rage was just as deadly as panic; it prevented rational thinking. Right then, that was what we needed the most. With my experience, I need to give my men the confidence they needed to get out of this mess.

I feared we were behind Russian lines, so I told my men that we needed to move very slowly, hopefully in the right direction. Adding up all the tactical factors, I figured we had the advantage. Right now the fog was befriending us through its capacity to hide our movements, as we had learned in the village earlier in the day. However, sounds seemed to travel further in the fog, so it was essential that we not make any noise. Because this was all new territory to the Russians, I suspected they would not be moving around much for fear of falling into a trench full of Germans. We had been over this territory before and had the advantage of knowing a little bit about our position.

Finally we reached the end of the trench and moved out into the frozen furrows of a plowed field. As we tried to cross, it was almost impossible to walk without stumbling or making noise. The fog had lifted slightly and I could see dark shadows in the distance. I guessed this was the village where we had encountered the tank earlier in the day. We made a broad circle around the village to avoid any Russians who might have taken shelter there for the night. At this point, I knew exactly where we were as well as the direction we needed to go to reach the *Feuerstellung*.

Shortly after midnight, we arrived back at the *Feuerstellung*, where I uncorked. I could not remember a time in my life when I had been so angry. How could anyone send us to the forward observation post when there was not a single soldier anywhere to be found in the trenches! I was beside myself with rage at these idiots, and angry at getting myself

into a position that could get me killed. I had to cool off, and at that moment I was in the right place to do that.

* * * * * * *

Our division began to pull back in a somewhat orderly manner that kept us between the Russians on both flanks. Other German units to our rear kept the line wide open to protect our retreat and avoid encirclement. Night after night, however, we would lie in the frozen snow with little to protect us from the bitter cold. Gradually, I began to suffer from the same injuries I had received on the Don Front. My legs and feet were freezing, and soon blisters and infection began to reappear on my feet. I needed medical attention.

I was sent away in a Red Cross van to a nearby hospital in Graudenz, about 70 miles south of Danzig. From there I transferred to another hospital further north and west, in Kolberg, on the Baltic Sea.

In Kolberg, a school gymnasium had been converted into a hospital. There were about 100 soldiers being treated for various wounds and injuries. Once again my body was scrubbed and cleaned, just as in Witzenhausen, but this time I was not embarrassed. A beautiful woman, who introduced herself as Utta, was caring for me. She turned out to be a medical doctor. She volunteered to work at this hospital several hours a day, and it was obvious she cared very deeply for her patients.

As my wounds healed, I was soon able to put my boots back on and walk. Utta asked me if I would like to see the city and the surrounding areas, and, of course, I said yes. I had learned that beautiful nurses and doctors seemed to have a profound effect on my recovery.

We walked on the sandy beaches of the Baltic Sea and talked of the places we knew; places like Rauschen, Cranz and Rositten. I told her about the white sand dunes of the Kurische Nehrung near my home. We came to enjoy each other's company immensely. It was cold, and large waves pounded the shoreline. Somewhere out there, I knew there were German ships ferrying women, children and wounded soldiers out of East Prussia.

I was so grateful that most of my family was safe. The end was drawing near in Tilsit. I thought about the people I knew who were still there, especially my father. I thought about the fears they must have, facing an uncertain future at the hands of angry Russians. On January 20, I learned that Tilsit had fallen to the Russians. I prayed that my father was alive and safe, but I feared the worst.

* * * * * *

As I lay in bed one night in late January 1945, I was awakened by activity next to me. A new patient had been brought in, and I rolled over and went back to sleep. In the morning, I awoke and looked over to see who my new neighbor might be. I was shocked to see a face that was white as the sheets and his lips were blue. He was wrapped in heavy blankets, and there was no sign of life whatsoever. I watched and waited for any indication that he might still be alive.

About an hour later, he opened his eyes. I smiled, and he smiled back.

"What happened to you?"

He said nothing and closed his eyes again. Several hours later he awakened, and apologized for the disturbance the night before. Of course, I was not offended, but very concerned for his well-being. Again I asked what had happened to him, and why was he here?

He told me his name was Heinz, and that he was a sailor aboard the passenger liner *Wilhelm Gustloff* that had been ferrying civilians and wounded soldiers from Danzig to Germany. The night before, his ship was en route to Germany with its navigation lights on and also marked clearly with a well-lit red cross on the side of the ship. Three Russian torpedoes had hit them just north of Leba, about 20 miles off the Pomeranian coast. He had been on the bridge standing watch when the ship was hit. He leaped from the bridge into the icy waters of the Baltic but had managed to pull himself up onto a floating object. It didn't take long for the ship to sink. The sea was calm, and the night was very dark. He estimated that maybe a few hundred people got off the ship. As he clung to his raft, he would occasionally hear what sounded like an empty bottle filling with water. He decided it was the sound of another survivor giving up and sinking into the frigid depths of the Baltic. Soon the area was filled with small boats, one of which rescued him from his precarious raft on the open sea.

"I think I was lucky this time," he said, as his eyes closed and he drifted off.

More than 6,000 civilians, soldiers and sailors went to the bottom that night – the largest single loss of life in maritime history.[2] Heinz was one of only a few that survived the sinking and the exposure. I later learned that it was Russian submarine *S-13* commanded by Captain Ivan Marinesko of the Soviet Navy that had committed this cowardly act, knowing full well who was aboard the *Wilhelm Gustloff*.[3]

* * * * * * *

One afternoon after our regular walk on the beach, Utta invited me to have something warm to drink at her tennis club, not far from the beach. Sitting in the clubhouse sipping hot chocolate, I asked her about the future. The Russians were less than 75 miles away. I told her it was time for her to pack her bags and move west. The Russians would not be kind to her, I explained. I didn't need to tell her what the worst possibilities might be.

Utta listened to me quietly, and soon tears began to roll down her cheeks. She turned away and for a long time looked out over the Baltic Sea. I was perplexed. Then she quietly and calmly responded. She explained that Kolberg was her home, and that she and her father were both doctors. They had an adequate supply of cyanide. They would not leave their home, and they would not leave their patients. This was their decision, and it would not change. With a big smile on her face, she asked me to change the subject.

We continued our daily walks on the beach, and I grew very close to her. I knew that the feelings were mutual, but we never talked of the future. By the end of February, it was time for me to return to the war. As I prepared to leave, I made one more attempt to convince her there was still time for her to escape. With tears in her eyes, she grabbed me and held me close, not wanting to let go. My heart was breaking, and I just could not understand or accept that our lives needed to part this way. It made no sense. Gradually, she let me go and looked into my eyes, saying more in her silence than anything she could ever have spoken. Then she kissed me gently, turned, and walked away, pausing once to turn back and wave. I never saw her again.

CHAPTER 14
ENDGAME

MY RESERVE UNIT headquarters had moved from Heilsburg, in East Prussia, to the city of Schwerin, just east of Hamburg. I remained in Schwerin for several weeks, waiting for new orders to the front. On March 18, Kolberg fell to the First Belorussian Front and the Polish 1st Army. I could only imagine what had become of Utta.

Most Germans realized the war was lost. The concerns we had now focused on surviving the war and hopefully surrendering to the British or Americans pressing from the west. Very few were willing to die for a cause that had failed them, or to which they had never paid any allegiance. Still, the rhetoric filled our ears, as did promises of new miracle weapons that would save Germany. The Nazis were beaten, Germany was crumbling by the minute, and Hitler was in denial in his fortified bunker in Berlin.

I mustered in full battle gear with several thousand other German troops of our newly formed regiment. We formed up to listen to our fearless commander tell us about our duties: to fight for the Führer and for the Fatherland. He also spoke of the new wonder weapons that would be at our disposal. I chuckled. I could hardly wait to see these weapons but seriously doubted that they existed. As I looked around me, I saw few soldiers who appeared to have been in battle. There were many young faces, very many old faces.

Finally, when the speech was over, our commander headed back to Schwerin and we headed to the train going to the front. Our fearless commander would not be joining us. What an inspiration he was to us all! It furthered my resolve to survive so I could return and find this coward and tell him what I really thought. Was he ready to die for the Führer? I thought not. I would later learn that many army commanders were now refusing to carry out ridiculous orders from Hitler that would result in the loss of German soldiers. Perhaps cooler heads were replacing the insanity that had gripped our country for so long. The Nazis were losing control, and fear was spreading within their ranks.

Our regiment was ordered to Stettin on the Oder River near the Baltic Sea. We would be facing the right flank of the First Belorussian Front, which was poised along the eastern bank of the Oder, ready to strike at Berlin.

* * * * * *

As mentioned earlier, an intense rivalry had developed between Marshal Zhukov of the First Belorussia front, and Marshal Koniev of the First Ukrainian Front.[1] I had fought soldiers under the command of each of them and found all of them to be formidable. Zhukov had earlier been promised the honor of taking Berlin; however, for several weeks Koniev had been advancing through the German Army like a hot knife through butter. He was bent on getting to Berlin first.

Stalin played both of these master warriors against each other rather effectively, and both were getting the maximum effort from their officers and men. From our point of view, these Russians were relentless and driven. They had rocked the Wehrmacht back on its heels and were now poised for the knockout blow. It was awesome and frightening to think about what was coming next. Of course, none of us were aware of this rivalry; we only saw the results.

By April of 1945, Zhukov had encountered more difficulty in getting to the Oder than he had expected. Stalin decided to make the game a little more interesting, so he gave Marshal Koniev a slight opportunity to get to Berlin first. He removed a line of demarcation that Koniev had previously been forbidden to cross, effectively barring him from Berlin.[2] Now the gate had opened and Koniev was charging hard from the southeast. Zhukov was furious, and quickly whipped his troops into shape for an all-out assault from the Northeast. The odds were still with Zhukov that he would reach Berlin first, but Stalin had stung his pride.

Covering Zhukov's right flank would be Marshal Rokossovsky's Second Belorussian Front that had just overrun East Prussia and Northern Poland, including Kolberg. Rokossovsky was ordered to clean out the Pomeranian threat.[3] Directly in his path was Stettin, and me.

* * * * * * *

I received a new assignment at Stettin. I was to be a liaison between the infantry regiment and the artillery battalion. This was all new to me and required several days to get organized. As we deployed ourselves into position, I looked for these new wonder weapons. Knowing full well they did not exist, I was not disappointed by the lies. What disappointed me, however, was surveying the weapons we did have. For the most part, our batteries consisted of outdated 105mm Howitzers with very few rounds of ammunition. The Rumanian Army on the Don Front had been better equipped than this! At least we had rocks. If we ran out of ammunition, we would just defend these bridgeheads by throwing rocks.

All of us knew the heavy artillery and ammunition had all been removed to Berlin to protect our brave Führer. We were expendable, and it was certain that our role in saving Hitler was to become grist in the tracks of Russian tanks. We just might slow them down – well, maybe for a few minutes anyway. As you can imagine, morale was not very high. The war would soon be over, and no one wanted to die now. We had gone through so much that we believed it was a miracle we were still alive. We needed to survive, and we needed to avoid capture by the Russians.

* * * * * * *

Stettin was a beautiful city of about 200,000 people on the Oder River. It had been an important seaport that connected the inland cities of central Europe to the sea. When we dug our trenches in the spring of 1945, it was hardly the first time that wars had come to this city. Stettin began as a settlement of Slavs in the 9th century and had gradually become a thriving center of commerce. In 1237, Stettin received its first municipal charter, and in 1251 it joined the Hanseatic League. It became the capital of Pomerania. In 1346, Pomeranian Dukes began to build its magnificent castle, which was completed in the 1700s. In 1648, Sweden invaded Pomerania, occupying Stettin and controlling the region until 1720, when the Prussians finally drove the Swedes back across the Baltic Sea. Since 1720, Stettin had been under the control of Germany. Unknown to us at the time, its postwar fate had already been sealed.[4]

On February 4, 1945, while I was recuperating in Kolberg, the last meeting between President Roosevelt, Prime Minister Winston Churchill and Premier Josef Stalin began at Yalta in the Crimea. During the conference, it was decided, among other things, that Stettin would become Polish after the war, which it remains to this day as the City of Szczecin. At the end of the war, Allied bombing had destroyed more than 60% of the city. Winston Churchill would later immortalize Stettin in his famous speech at Fulton College in Missouri, when he would state, "From Stettin in the Baltic to Trieste in the Adriatic, an Iron Curtain has descended across the continent."[5] We were fighting over the drawstrings of that curtain.

* * * * * * *

When we arrived in Stettin, the streets were deserted; not a soul could be found anywhere. Fully furnished apartments had been abandoned. There were no signs of looting, but I was sure the Russians would take care of that. My soldiers and I wanted to live; we wanted nothing more to do with this war. We had been ordered to protect Stettin as a fortress and to frustrate the Russians from crossing the Oder River. We had received little to defend this city and, to us, the handwriting was on the wall. We would do our best until we could do no more. At that point, I figured it would once again be every man for himself.

At a briefing with some of our staff members, I was ordered to take a team of eight men across the river. We were to move to the east side of the Oder and north to the last bridge before the river opens into Stettin Harbor. We reached the river by late afternoon. We then had to cross a bridge about 100 meters long. It was very exposed, and gunfire and mortar shells were hitting all around us. One by one, we each crossed the bridge, diving for cover several times. Once on the east side of the river, we moved north and found a large building near our assigned position. Inside was a well-furnished, comfortable apartment where we set up our equipment.

Stettin Harbor was filled with several sunken ships. Oil slicks with their rainbow-reflected patterns covered floating debris and other bloated objects we really didn't care to identify. Smoke stacks and masts, with block and tackle hanging askew from the yardarms, marked the location of sunken ships and boats that blocked passage both into the harbor and up the river. The destruction was depressing, and the smell of death was everywhere. Occasional explosions from mortar fire and the rat-tat-tat of small arms fire kept us on our toes. However, there were no serious engagements with the Russians.

In mid-April I was summoned to regimental headquarters where I was escorted into a room and met by the regimental commander. He took me to a large map hanging on the wall. He pointed to a location south of Stettin where he said Russians had crossed the Oder River and had established a bridgehead on the western side. This position was of vital strategic importance because of its proximity to the Stettin-Berlin autobahn. The commander explained the potential danger. If the Russians got enough troops and equipment across the bridge and controlled this area, they would gain access to the autobahn. Hitler's engineering marvel would therefore assist in his rapid demise. The Russians would move rapidly down the autobahn and flank the city from the north.

Our job was to push the bridgehead back across the Oder and prevent access to the autobahn. I learned the counteroffensive would begin at midnight, first with an artillery barrage that would last for about 30 minutes. After this initial artillery barrage, I was to direct the artillery to the east and west sides of the bridge. This would allow the infantry to destroy the soldiers dug in on the west side of the river while preventing reinforcements from crossing the bridge by my continuing artillery fire. I received new maps of the area that had clearly marked grids with numbered squares. In each numbered square were four quarters, labeled a, b, c, and d. This was far more useful for calling artillery fire than any map I had used before. Each battery in the area had the same map and would all coordinate easily with my calls for fire.

I had my orders. I gathered my team of eight and we headed south. Russian artillery rounds were falling on the main roads. High explosive rounds were destroying everything in most of the villages we passed. The same fierce shelling that we had experienced in Silesia and Poland was now hitting German soil. The reality of the Red Army had arrived at Germany's doorstep. We stayed off the roads and out of the villages, crossing fields and back roads to avoid the Russian artillery. Still, the going was rough, and Russian spotters never failed to direct fire at us whenever they saw us. The whistle of an incoming round sent us scrambling for cover in trees, ditches and anything else that would protect us from the exploding shrapnel. The twisted hot metal fragments whistled through the trees, shredding leaves and branches. Sometimes they landed on us, burning holes in our uniforms and occasionally in our skin.

Late in the evening, the sun had just set, but its rays shining above the penumbra of oncoming twilight revealed large, dark clouds in the east that were threatening rain. I prayed there would be no rain that night; rain could create confusion and lower visibility. I did not want any of our troops hit by friendly fire simply because I could not see to mark the proper target. As we moved on it got darker, then – finally – I sighted our objective: a large gravel pit that would be our spotting position.

I found the infantry commander a very affable major. He was glad to see us and made sure that we had everything we needed. His troops were in foxholes surrounding the edge of the gravel pit. I spoke with a few of them, inquiring how close the Russians were to the gravel pit. One turned to me and said, "About 50 yards." I was astonished. This was awfully close!

In the bottom of the pit there were a few bunkers. I told my men to set up our equipment in the largest one, which would serve as our command post. Soon three more officers arrived to support my team and ensure that everything was in order. They checked and rechecked communications and the battle plan, then made sure that everyone understood their duty. Both my team and I were ready, and we had excellent communications with headquarters. As we waited for midnight, the infantry commander came to me again. He told me he had only 50% of his normal strength, and requested that we provide as much artillery support as possible to protect his troops. I told him we would give him all we had. He smiled and turned back to his troops. I didn't have the heart to tell him how low we were on ammunition. I think he already knew the hopelessness of our situation. We had orders to push this bridgehead back across the Oder. We had the courage and will to carry out our orders; what we lacked were the tools to do our job. We were expendable.

Promptly at midnight, the whole western horizon lit up with flashes of light. A deep thunderous roar reached us moments later, followed quickly by the whistle of incoming artillery rounds. Flares shot up over

the Russian position that covered an area about three miles square.
Explosions rocked the Russians out of their sleep, and for the next half-
hour they scrambled for cover. We could not yet see the effect of our
bombardment but hoped against hope that it was working.

At half-past midnight, we called to readjust the fire toward the river
to encourage the Russians to cross back over the Oder and allow our
infantry to move into the bridgehead area to mop up after the retreating
Russians. As this phase of the operation continued, I sensed there was
a weakening of our artillery attack. The time between explosions
gradually widened and the number of shots dropped dramatically. What
I had feared had come to pass. We were running out of ammunition.

Our infantry moved out, meeting little resistance. Had the Russians
fallen back? Occasionally we saw a flare, or another artillery round
exploded near the bridge. It was so dark. It was impossible to know
what was going on. All we could do was sit nervously and hope that our
assault had succeeded.

By 4:00 a.m. the artillery barrage had stopped completely. As I
looked about, I saw there were plenty of rocks in the gravel pit. We
chuckled nervously at the thought of having to use them. Gradually, our
infantry troops returned in the predawn light and slumped into their
foxholes. The assault was over. The Russians had been able to bring up
several tanks and heavy artillery before our attack began. There was no
way that our light infantry could push them back across the Oder. Our
mission had failed, and we were out of ammunition.

The morning of April 18 dawned with a cool breeze and bright sunshine. It was so pleasant, but I wondered seriously if I would survive the day. I called my troops together in our bunker to tell them that retreat was unavoidable. There was no way we could hold this position, and the Russians were only moments away. I pulled out my map and showed them a road that led north by northwest. Between the gravel pit and the road was a field about 500 yards wide that we would have to cross to get to the road. I told them to spread out and run like the wind. If anyone got hit, I told the men to make sure anyone who fell was picked up or dragged along. I told them I would bring up the rear and make sure they would all make it. We were now living our lives from minute to minute. Since we knew that death was stalking us, the tension was incredible.

As we prepared to leave our bunker, I was finishing a conversation with headquarters calling for fire on our position to keep the Russians back. Sitting in the corner of our bunker, I heard a soldier outside yelling at us that Russian tanks were entering the north end of the gravel pit. Most of my men went rushing outside to look for these tanks. Suddenly there was a flash and an incredible concussion as a tank round hit our bunker. Six men were lying in a heap, covered with blood, dirt and concrete dust and moaning in agony. Only one other private and I were in one piece. Again I called for suppressing fire.

It was a mess. Blood was flowing everywhere with its sickening, sweet odor. I was starting to panic but quickly forced myself to calm down. If it was our time to die, then it was our time to die. But until I was dead, I had to keep working. I could not leave these wounded men in the gravel pit. I sent my private to one of the other nearby bunkers where there were other artillery troops. He dashed out of the bunker for help. Meanwhile, I examined the wounds and started bandaging them as best I could. I was counting the minutes and praying that help would come soon.

Outside, the suppressing fire from our 88mm guns were keeping the Russians down. Time ticked by so slowly. I feared that my life was about to end, but I had to keep working. Then the infantry commander came by to let me know they were pulling back. My situation was looking bleaker. As he bade me farewell, I'm sure he believed I would soon be finished.

Finally, after the longest ten minutes of my life, my private returned with five others. I again radioed for heavy suppressing fire. We then grabbed the wounded and headed out of the bunker. I brought up the rear as we ran for the western rim of the gravel pit. My private and I were now on our own, the wounded having been evacuated to another bunker. I wondered if any of them would survive.

When we reached the western rim, we paused and studied what was in front of us. The field was about 500 yards across and covered with wheat about a foot high. Both of us were carrying radios on our back that might offer extra protection. After discussing our alternatives, both of us agreed that crossing the field was our only choice. The tension was incredible as we both realized the odds of our surviving this run were stacked high against us.

I took off first, in a dead run. Then the turkey shoot began. Bullets were zinging by my ears and kicking up dust all around me. I was sprinting as fast as I could. My thighs were burning, and my lungs felt like they would explode. I could feel my heart thumping wildly. Sweat was pouring down my face, dripping off my nose and chin. Although my eyes were burning and blurred from the sweat streaming down my forehead, I could see the road coming closer. I wanted so desperately to live; I was giving every ounce of effort I could muster. I had never been so frightened in my entire life.

Mortar rounds began landing around us. Trying to dodge the explosions as much as possible, we both kept running. And then I was there! I was up the embankment and across the road first. The ditch on the other side would give us a few moments of cover and rest. As I turned, I saw the private start up the embankment just as a mortar round hit nearby. A jagged piece of shrapnel tore into his neck and he was down. I quickly dragged him to cover, relieved to see that he was still alive. I managed to stop most of the bleeding and bandage his wound. Carrying him over my shoulder, I went in search of a first aid station. It wasn't too long before we got to one, and I was grateful to be able to leave my private in good hands.

Somehow, I found my regimental staff. After I reported eight casualties and the loss of all my equipment, I was told not to worry because there was no more ammunition to fight this war.

"So is the war over?"

"No! We must keep fighting!"

For the next several days, I moved west with the regimental staff, one step ahead of the Russians. The infantry units covered our retreat, but I knew this could not continue at the same pace or we would be overrun. The prospect of going back to Russia was all the motivation I needed to survive, so my mind was considering choices by the minute. What I wanted to do more than anything was keep moving west to find British and American lines. Everywhere units were falling apart; soldiers were fleeing in every direction. But I cautioned myself; I could be shot if I deserted. I had no intention of even considering such a thing – yet.

One night I had the opportunity to overhear a briefing of our regimental staff officers. They all agreed that since there was no ammunition left, it was impossible to fight the enemy. So it was useless to remain and be captured. I quietly left the building and returned to my men. I explained to them the war was over, there was nothing more that we could do. Our staff officers were leaving; their bags were packed. I suggested it was time for us to leave as well. If anyone disagreed with me, they were welcome to report me. But none of them disagreed, and all decided it was time for each of us to make it to safety. We shook hands and, one by one, left our shelter and disappeared into the night. I left my battle gear behind. Only a few important items, including my small-caliber pistol, went with me. My days as a fighting soldier for the Reich were over. Now I had to survive.

CHAPTER 15
SURRENDER

As THE DRAMA of Germany's collapse played out on the world stage, I was with thousands of other German civilians and soldiers who were fleeing along the road to the west. Some carried their belongings wrapped in blankets slung over their shoulders. Others pulled wagons and handcarts. Some children rode atop the carts, their faces filled with looks of confusion and hunger. Others walked beside a parent or sibling, clinging to their hands in fear. Interspersed with this river of humanity were army trucks and equipment – broken-down vehicles pushed to the side, and an occasional corpse of a refugee who could go no further lined the road.

There was very little conversation; no one even smiled. Each of us was on our own, slogging along without food, without water, without sleep. Not even the children cried. You might expect that under these conditions children would be crying and screaming. I suspected they were all too tired, all too hungry. It was as if they had cried all the tears out of their eyes: nothing remained but empty stares. These heartbreaking images of the ravaged remnants of the war remained with me for the rest of my life.

One afternoon, as we approached a small town not far from Neubrandenburg, we could see up ahead that the road was blocked by a group of SS soldiers, maybe the Gestapo as well. I stayed back at a safe distance to see what was going on. There were several Wehrmacht soldiers in this march to the west. It appeared that they were being pulled out, given new rifles, and assigned to groups marching back to the east. Those who refused earned a place in the trees, hanging by the neck with a sign saying "I am a deserter."[1]

They were executing soldiers who had fought bravely for almost four years on the Eastern Front so these rear echelon cowards could beat up Jews and terrorize the country. These soldiers had suffered at the hands of Hitler's incompetent leadership, endured incredibly harsh conditions, and lost friends and comrades because of Hitler's moronic orders to "fight to the end." For what purpose? There was no shortage of inhumanity, blind stupidity and cowardice among these Nazis. I hated them and everything for which they stood. The greatest satisfaction was in knowing that it would soon be over for them. The only bullets they ever fired killed Germans. Hopefully they would use their last bullets on themselves, so they could join Hitler in Nazi Nirvana.

Years of experience as an artillery spotter had trained me to observe everything, a skill I practiced from my position in some trees away from the road. As I watched this roadblock, I noticed that wounded soldiers were getting through; in fact, they were the only ones allowed to proceed. The conclusion was obvious. If I were wounded, I had a chance of making it to the west. Otherwise, I was doomed to return to the east for certain death or capture. Since I was not wounded, the only way I was going to become wounded was to shoot myself. The idea was absurd! I could not believe that I would ever seriously consider such a crazy idea. But as I continued to watch, I realized that, indeed, the only way I would get through this roadblock was with a wound, a wound that was either actually serious or at least appeared to be. The whole idea made me wonder if I was losing my mind!

As it got dark, I decided I would ponder this dilemma through the night and decide in the morning. I found a comfortable place to lie down, but sleep eluded me all night. I tossed and turned in fitful attempts to sleep, my mind racing with thoughts, arguments and counter-arguments. There was no answer for this problem. I tried to calm down and listen for the still, small voice inside me that would know what I should do. Unfortunately, my head filled with so much noise that this small voice could not be heard.

The sky grew light as dawn approached. It was the morning of April 30, 1945. I had decided my only chance was to go through with this plan. I got up as the morning sunlight was just hitting the tops of the trees. I walked back into the forest, listening carefully to ensure that no one was around. I soon found a spot surrounded by pine trees and thick underbrush. The only sounds were those of the birds singing in the trees amid the soft shafts of sunlight filtering down through the forest canopy. It was unreal!

I now felt calm, reassured that my plan was OK. I pulled the left sleeve of my uniform back and studied my arm. I knew that I would have to avoid any large arteries or veins, and that I should avoid shattering the bone. The bullet needed to exit cleanly so I would not be carrying any more poison around with me than I had to. I decided that I would shoot through the fleshy upper side of my left forearm, about three or four inches below the elbow. I pulled a gauze roll from my jacket, laid the muzzle of the pistol against the gauze and placed the gauze against my arm. And there I sat.

My hands shook, my heart was pounding and I was crying. What was I doing here? This was insane! I could not pull the trigger. Voices were screaming in my ears; visions of my family passed before me. Why was I afraid? I had endured far worse than this. I gazed into the tops of the trees with soft angelic sunlight falling all around me, listening to the beautiful melody sung by the birds that were fluttering from branch to branch. What did those silly birds know about me, this lonely soldier afraid to do this simple thing?

WHAM!

The birds stopped singing. The pistol fell to the ground. Suddenly the world was spinning, and I collapsed. I felt a sharp sting in my arm. As I regained my senses, I saw that my whole sleeve was soaked in blood. The roll of gauze lay on the ground, black from the powder burns. The bullet had gone through my arm as I had hoped. I let the wound continue to bleed, both to clean it out and to allow it to soak more into my uniform. I then pulled another roll of gauze out and wrapped the wound tightly. After making a sling out of a third roll of gauze, I laid down to rest. The birds renewed their chorus while the sheltering trees and bushes around me stood guard. I remained there for the next several hours.

Early in the afternoon, it was time to rejoin the refugees on the road. I made my way into the ragged formation of wounded soldiers and refugees, finding a group of wounded men to accompany. Because the Russians were very close, the number of wounded men had increased dramatically. Behind us I could hear the sounds of war, which I had come to know so well over the previous four years. Yes, they were very close.

As we drew nearer to the SS checkpoint, my heart was pounding and my head was spinning. I was afraid I might pass out. Then it was my turn. The SS officer looked me over, from top to bottom. I was a mess. I was covered in dirt from my days at Stettin, my face was haggard and unshaven, my whole left arm was soaked in blood, my uniform was torn, and I am sure my odor was not pleasant either. He then stared coldly into my face with this Nazi look of superiority and hatred. I felt I was looking at the Devil himself.

"You, sir, are badly in need of a cleanup. See that building over there? It is a hospital. Go check yourself in."

"Yes, sir!"

Ja, sure I will. I thought to myself as I moved slowly away from the checkpoint. I just kept on the road going west. I don't think anyone noticed that I walked right on past the hospital; I don't think anyone cared. I didn't stop all night. I just kept moving forward, ahead of the roar of the Red Army behind us. We were not gaining any ground. To be sure, the Russians were getting closer. I was about 30 miles east of Schwerin, my destination. During my days there in March I had made friends with several residents of that town. I was hoping to find some shelter and food, and possibly to join with people moving toward American lines.

At daybreak I was exhausted. I had not slept in days, nor had I eaten in about a week. I was losing blood and desperately needed at least a short rest. As we passed a farmhouse about 20 miles out of Schwerin, I noticed some straw caps near the barn and decided to rest there for a while. It was a beautiful spring day, marred only by the boom and rattle of the approaching Russians and the unbelievable river of humanity fleeing to the west. I rested just for a bit, realizing it was really no time to dally.

By nightfall, I had arrived in Schwerin and found my friends. I was so exhausted that after tending to my wound, I collapsed into a deep sleep. I planned to get medical attention the next day, including perhaps a tetanus shot. I would then consider what options I had to get to American lines.

* * * * * *

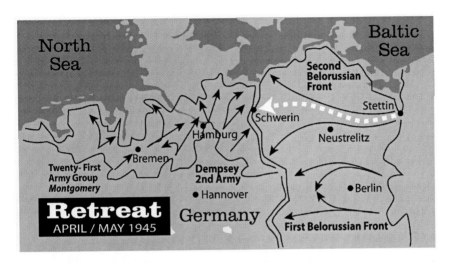

Schwerin, the capital of Mecklenburg, was a beautiful city. It sat among several beautiful lakes. On a nearby island, one of the dukes of Mecklenburg had built a fairy tale castle in the 1800s. Intellectual life had thrived in Mecklenburg in the 15th century; thus, Schwerin had long been referred to as the Florence of the north.[2] The castle and most of the older medieval buildings had, so far, survived the war. However, with the Russians marching closer from the east, everyone feared that a Russian bombardment would destroy everything.

I awakened early and set off to get medical attention for my arm at a local hospital. En route back to my friends' home, I stopped at a Navy supply depot and picked up a dark-blue Navy uniform, a favorite choice among many soldiers. We did not want to be caught out of uniform, and it was appropriate to shed the filthy, bloody uniform I had been wearing.

As I walked through the city center, the eerie quiet told me something was up. I saw people pulling their window shutters closed. Then I heard the familiar sound of tanks. Were they Russian? Where were they coming from? It was impossible to tell as sounds echoed from every direction.

I hoped and prayed that they were not Russians. As I was hiding behind buildings, trying to see whose tanks had entered the city, an older woman came out of her apartment and asked me to come with her. It wasn't safe on the streets, and I needed to get out of my Army uniform. She took me into her apartment, telling me to change. She then cut my filthy Army uniform into pieces and burned everything. I put on the blue uniform, and we sat and waited, and waited.

The sound of the tanks grew closer. It was obvious they were heading into the center of town. I was nervous. I was scared. My options were over. There was no more escape. My entire future rested on this moment and would depend completely on whose tank was at that instant going to drive past the old woman's apartment window. Then it was there, a long tank barrel in drab olive green, and then the most beautiful sight I had ever seen - the big white star of the American Army painted on the side of a Sherman tank!

In an instant the tension of four years of war unwound inside me. I laughed, I cried, I jumped up and down like a little kid. The war was over. I would not be going back to Russia, I was no longer subject to Nazis, I would never again carry arms into war. I fell to my knees and thanked God I had been spared. Never had I felt so many emotions at one time. I couldn't contain myself. Nobody could.

There had been no resistance to the Allied occupation of Schwerin. Not a single shot had been fired. It was late in the afternoon of May 2, 1945, when Lieutenant-General Sir Miles Dempsey and his British 2nd Army, together with American and Canadian units, stopped. This was the easternmost allied penetration into Germany in this sector. The Russians had also stopped their forward motion; only the refugees were being allowed to continue westward.

When I saw other Germans coming into the streets, welcoming both American and British soldiers, I bid this kind woman good-bye and headed back to my friends' home. Once more, we exulted in our good fortune. The relief was enormous to everyone. As it got dark, the lights of the city turned on for the first time in years, and we cried tears of joy. It was so beautiful, so memorable - a sight I will never forget, a feeling I will always remember. An enormous weight had lifted from my shoulders.

We were all required to remain inside from 7:00 p.m. to 7:00 a.m., a rule to which none of us objected. For the first night in a very long time, there was no artillery fire booming in the distance. There were no air raid sirens, no sounds of war whatsoever. It was quiet - quiet and peaceful, so very peaceful. I slept like a baby and, over the next several days, became rested and regained my strength.

My thoughts then turned to my family; it was time for me to find them. I knew they were near Freiberg, and Saxony was a long way from Mecklenberg. Since I had been walking for the entire war, I resolved to walk to Freiberg. When I shared my plan with my friends and their neighbors, everyone objected, warning that I would never get there. All transportation was out of order, and they urged me to wait until the trains started running again.

None of us knew that Germany had been partitioned into various zones of occupation, nor did we have any inkling of what travel documents were required. Unknown to me, a pass from the local military command was needed to travel within the American occupied zone and another pass to travel in other zones. I was ignorant of where one zone ended and another began. Worst of all, I had no clue that Freiberg was then in the Russian zone. All I knew was that Freiberg was 250 miles southwest of Schwerin and that I was prepared to walk the distance. Finally my friends and neighbors understood that I was going to go, whether they liked it or not. So they set about helping me get on my way. One neighbor brought over an old bicycle that was in good condition. This would make my trip much easier. The next morning, I waved good-bye to my friends and began my journey. Other than the few sandwiches my friends had fixed, I carried very little.

It was another beautiful spring day, and the countryside was gorgeous. I daydreamed about seeing my family again. I could see my mother taking me into her arms, so surprised that I had survived the war. At that time they had no idea where I was, or even if I was alive. As

I pedaled along, I felt like I was in good shape; my arm was healing well and I expected to be in Freiberg within a few days. I continued to head south along the main road in blissful ignorance.

As I pedaled past a farm field, some American G.I.s appeared from nowhere on horseback and asked me to stop. They asked where I was going, but of course my English was not very good. I tried to tell them I was going home to my family in Freiberg. Then they told me if I kept going on this road, I was about to cross into the Russian Zone. I had no idea what the Russian Zone was, but it was enough to convince me not to go any farther. I politely thanked these Americans and turned to find another way.

Pedaling back up the road, I came to an intersection where American M.P.s were directing all traffic down a single gravel road. I was confused, and soon found myself being herded into an old German airfield that was rapidly filling up with German POWs. I did not want to be here! I walked slowly along the gravel road trying to figure out what to do. I had no wish to be a POW sitting out in the sun at this airfield all day. The administration building was only two hundred yards ahead, so I had to do something quickly. Was there any way to escape?

I looked around and saw there were no guards along the road. On the right-hand side there was an eight-foot-high fence, which in some places did not reach the ground. Where it crossed a ditch, there was about two feet of open space underneath. I figured I could toss the bicycle over the top and then roll under the fence. Another check of my surroundings assured me there were still no guards along the road. It did appear that guards and machine guns had been placed on the flat roof of the administration building. However, I felt I was still too far away for them to notice me. Besides, they all seemed to be captivated by a strange American game going on in front of the building. It involved the Americans wearing big gloves and pounding them while a small white ball flew around between them. Whatever it was, the guards and sentries seemed to be enjoying it.

I checked one more time and then made my move. Whoosh! Up and over the top of the fence went my bicycle, coming down with a thump on the other side. I was under the fence in a flash, I picked up my bike, and in no time became like a wild moose charging through the underbrush into the forest. When I finally stopped and looked back, it appeared that no one had seen my flight or even cared that I had escaped.

Into the forest I went, carrying my bicycle and running as fast as I could. After a while, I stopped to catch my breath and listen to see if anyone was following me. Although it was quiet and peaceful again, I decided I had done enough running. I didn't like this feeling of fear, as if I were a hunted deer. I resolved to return to my friends in Schwerin and become better prepared by learning about the zones of occupation before I tried again. Though the war was over, these were still dangerous times. I couldn't simply wander off in blissful ignorance anymore.

By late afternoon I was back with my friends in Schwerin. They all laughed when I told them of my adventure, and soon the whole neighborhood was abuzz with stories of my escape. The next few weeks were spent waiting for another opportunity, learning all I could about travel in postwar Germany.

CHAPTER 16
MY ODYSSEY

DURING THE FIRST weeks after the end of the war, there were units of the Western Allied forces – mostly British, American and French – scattered all over the western half of Germany. The Russians, on the other hand, occupied most of the states east of the Elbe River.

The issue of governing a defeated Germany had been an agenda item in every conference of Allied leaders since Churchill and Roosevelt met at Ship Harbor, Newfoundland, aboard the USS Augusta (CA-31) between August 9 and 12, 1941.[1] Almost four years later, the Potsdam Declaration was issued on August 2, 1945, in the last conference of the Grand Alliance leaders. The Potsdam Declaration became the blueprint for administering Germany under Allied occupation, which continued for several years after the war.[2]

One of the chief aims of the Potsdam Declaration was to eliminate German militarism and to destroy the Nazi Party. All Nazi organizations were disbanded, which included organizations like the SS, the SA, and the Gestapo. Further, all Nazi laws that had discriminated based on race, religion, creed or politics were abolished. Freedom of speech, the press, and religion were guaranteed. Nazis were to be removed from public office, although in many cases this was impossible because there was no one qualified to take over the responsibilities of certain offices.[3]

Political administration within the government was generally decentralized, with more power and responsibility given to state and local governments. The Allies did not allow a central government for Germany and instead administered certain international functions of state under the Allied Control Council.[4]

The demilitarization of Germany included the removal of the industrial ability to make war. As a result, many factories were disassembled and moved away. The Russians saw this as justifiable reparations for the Russian industry destroyed by the Germans. The Russians were able to satisfy some of their reparation claims by removing industrial equipment and factories to the Soviet Union and by seizing German assets in certain central and eastern European countries.[5]

The most notable and familiar result of the administration of the Allied Control Council involved placing Nazi leaders on trial in Nuremberg for war crimes. The Allies had announced as early as 1942 that they intended to prosecute the leaders of Germany for crimes against mankind. Eventually, 22 major figures in the Nazi leadership were tried; 12 were sentenced to death, three were acquitted and the rest sentenced to prison terms ranging from 10 years to life.[6]

The Potsdam Declaration essentially returned Germany's boundaries to those that had existed on December 31, 1937, before Hitler had begun his annexation of the Sudetenland in Czechoslovakia and effected the *Anschluss* of Austria in 1938. There were a few exceptions to this, including the loss of German territory to Poland east of the Oder-Niesse line, where I had been fighting at the end of the war. Germany also lost my homeland, East Prussia, to Russia.[7]

The Potsdam Declaration created four different zones and established separate administration of each zone by one of the four major allies of the Grand Alliance. France administered half of Baden-Wurttemberg, Rhineland-Palatinate, and Saarland, all of which were along the southern border between France and Germany. The Americans governed the other half of Baden-Wurttemberg, Bavaria and Hesse. The British administered the northwestern states of North Rhine-Westphalia, Lower Saxony, Schleswig-Holstein and the small portion of Mecklenberg in which I was located at Schwerin. The Russians occupied the larger portion of Mecklenberg, Brandenberg, Saxony-Anhalt, Thuringia and Saxony, where my family was living near the city of Freiberg.[8]

The intent of the Potsdam Declaration was that all Germans were to be treated the same, no matter in which zone they lived. As a matter of practicality, however, such was not the case. The French favored a decentralized government that they hoped would result in several small, loosely associated states, similar to conditions before Bismarck's unification of Germany into the Second Reich in 1871. France had thrived in a Europe where there was a lack of organization among the German-speaking states, and it longed to return to such a politically and economically favorable climate. The Russians were the opposite of the French, wanting instead a strong central government that they could influence, control and govern, similar to the Soviet form of government. The British also favored a centralized state, but not to the extreme of the Russians. The Americans wanted to create a federal state in Germany, and thus organized the governments in Bavaria, Hesse and Baden-Wurttemberg along much the same lines as a state government in the United States. Gradually, the differences in each zone had to adjust and become compatible with one another. However, in the summer of 1945, there was still a lot of confusion.[9]

* * * * * * *

By the summer of 1945, each of the four major members of the Grand Alliance consolidated control of their respective "spheres of influence," which had the immediate result of restricting travel. Without permission from the proper authorities, travel was strictly forbidden. Further, as I had learned in my ill-fated venture in May, the lines of demarcation between zones were not clearly marked. It was entirely possible to cross accidentally into a different Allied zone without the proper credentials for travel, and find yourself interned.

So there I sat in Schwerin, a lovely town, but far from home. I had not communicated with my family in almost a year, and I was eager to find them. For all they knew, I was dead.

One dark night, sometime after midnight, I heard a knock at my window, which faced into the backyard. Opening it, I discovered a man who was asking if he could come inside. He was obviously violating the strict curfew, and was in imminent danger of being shot.

I did not recognize this dashing fellow as he stepped into my room. He was wearing a leather vest and looked like a German pilot, which he turned out to be. He introduced himself as Hein, explaining that he was a close friend of the family with whom I was staying. As a German fighter pilot, he had served at the airfield near Schwerin when the war ended, after which he had been interned at the same POW camp into which I had almost stumbled. He had just escaped and, like me, longed to return to his home.

Hein was from Lauterbach, which lay in the rolling hills of Hesse, northeast of Frankfurt. He wanted me to join him in his journey home. From Lauterbach, it would not be difficult to reach Freiberg. We talked late into the night, sharing our experience over the last few years. Gradually, the whole house awakened and joined us. When we had run out of things to talk about, it was almost dawn.

I committed myself to this plan with my new friend Hein. As a pilot, he had become familiar with the land around Schwerin and was confident that he could get us on the road in the right direction. We were both itching to get underway, but there were still several obstacles we had to overcome. The most important was securing proper travel credentials. Next, we had to figure out how to cross to the west side of the Elbe River. Finally, we had to prepare ourselves for a journey of almost 200 miles by foot to Lauterbach. There was still no public transportation available anywhere in Germany. None of this deterred us, so we quickly set about solving these problems.

Securing the proper travel credentials was the most daunting task we faced. Since both of us were now escapees from this internment camp, asking permission from the Americans did not seem advisable. One afternoon while we were pondering the problem, I happened by chance to meet a fellow who had the proper credentials. He allowed me to inspect his travel document, which consisted of a typewritten page that read something like the following:

> Name:
> To whom it may concern.
> The bearer of this permit has
> permission to travel
> from_____ to_____
> Signed by
> Edward D. Midgley
> Captain, U.S. Army
> Schwerin Military Command

I secured a typewriter and we practiced until we were able to sign Captain Midgley's signature perfectly. Now that we had our travel permits and everything else in readiness, we decided to leave Schwerin the following morning. Again our friends prepared us well, offering food supplies with their best wishes.

We decided to stick to the less traveled back roads, which were not likely to have checkpoints and roadblocks. Our first stop would be the small town of Hagenow, about 15 miles southwest of Schwerin. Here we planned to spend our first night before continuing to Hitzacker, a small village on the west side of the Elbe River which was about 15 miles as the crow flies. However, following the undulating back roads from Hagenow, it would turn out to be a walk of about 30 miles.

Walking from Hagenow to Hitzacker, we were on a country road with deep forests on both sides. Since it had rained the night before, the air was fresh and clean. There was little traffic on the road, although once in a while an American Army jeep or truck would come by. So we walked on the shoulder, hiding quickly in the roadside bushes or trees every time we heard the sound of an oncoming vehicle.

Because no German vehicles were allowed to travel on these roads, the Americans had no traffic with which to contend. So they would zip up and down these roads at very high speeds, as if they were driving race cars in a Grand Prix. Their rapid approach sometimes created problems for us.

On one particular occasion, a jeep came around a corner very fast, giving us little time to get off the road. As we scrambled into the trees, we heard the driver slow down and stop. From our hiding place about 30 yards from the road, we stopped to see what he would do. To our amazement, he pulled his jeep off the road and started into the forest! Was this guy crazy? We moved deeper into the forest and hid ourselves under some thick brush. There was no way the jeep could follow us. Finally he gave up, roared back onto the highway, and took off fast in the same direction from which he had come.

Hein and I looked at each other, both thinking the same thing. We could not continue along this road because it was certain the driver of the jeep was going for help and would return to look for us. So we hiked deeper into the forest, traveling in a southerly direction.

Before long, we came to a farmhouse. We explained to the owner that we were trying to get home and asked him if we could spend the night in his barn. Both he and his wife were sympathetic to our cause. He warned us to stay away from the roads until we passed a nearby POW camp since the Americans patrolled all of these roads continuously. That night the farmer's wife fixed us one of the most wonderful meals I had eaten in years. It was so kind of these people to help us without knowing who we were or what we were up to. After dinner they put us up in the barn for a comfortable rest in the hayloft.

The next morning, the farmer woke us early, bringing us some clothing to make us look like farm laborers. After a wonderful breakfast and a fond farewell from his wife, our new friend loaded us onto his hay wagon and handed us pitchforks and old hats. We then drove lazily down a back road that took us past the POW camp and south of the area patrolled by the Americans. He finally dropped us off on a road which he said the Americans rarely patrolled. It would take us safely to the Elbe. After we expressed to him our deep gratitude, our friend passed from our lives forever, having helped us unconditionally and without any hesitation. I have never forgotten his kindness.

We walked along this road for the rest of the day, avoiding possible areas of exposure, and by nightfall found a safe place to sleep. The following morning we arrived at the majestic Elbe River, 150 yards wide, with a deep, fast-moving current. The prospect of crossing this river was intimidating, and we certainly had no delusions about swimming it. We were not far from Hitzacker. Looking up and down the river, we saw there were several fishermen and boat people living along the bank. We approached several of them, asking if they would take us across. All of them refused, saying the other side of the Elbe was now in a British Zone, and the British would cause them intolerable grief if they were caught taking us across.

It was a beautiful Sunday morning. Since we had no luck finding a trip across the river, we just laid in the grass on the bank of the river and soaked in the warm sunshine. We relaxed, listening to the song of a nearby meadowlark and enjoying the pleasant view of the Elbe. Suddenly, out of nowhere, came an American soldier riding on a horse that was obviously too small for him. It was the most comical sight I had seen in a long time. He looked like Don Quixote astride Rocinante, his legs flapping in and out against the side of this poor beast, spurring it on to capture two errant knights.

"What are you two doing here?"

I was struggling to keep my composure, biting my lip to keep from laughing. I could tell that Hein was also having trouble keeping a straight face.

"Who are you?" he repeated.

We handed him our travel permits. After studying them closely, he seemed satisfied, turned his mount, and disappeared just as quickly as he had appeared.

We remained there for a few moments longer before deciding it might be wise to find a hiding spot before another American showed up to take us away. Just as we were about to head into the woods, we noticed an old man push a rowboat into the river on the opposite bank. As he started rowing toward us, Hein and I could not believe this possible stroke of good luck. We turned back to the river and met this old fellow as he arrived.

"Would you like to cross the river?"

Both of us blurted out "Yes!" at the same time.

"All right then, grab the oars and keep rowing!"

So off we went into a strong current, Hein and I pulling on the oars and our new friend guiding us with the rudder. Soon we were across the river, once again beholden to the kindness of someone we had never met and likely would never see again. We expressed our gratitude and headed off toward Hitzacker.

We were now in the British Zone. As we approached Hitzacker, I saw British soldiers for the first time. They were marching briskly up and down the main street, swinging their arms as only British soldiers can do. It was beautiful to watch. I particularly enjoyed the British officers who barked commands and snapped their swagger sticks under their arm. These were very professional-looking soldiers, and we admired their drill for a long time. Finally, it was time to move on, so we headed out of town in a south-by-southwest direction, once again sticking to the back roads. In this zone, however, we had smooth sailing. The British never stopped us. Each day it seemed we moved a little faster, and Hein's excitement grew by the minute. He was like a horse headed for the barn. We reached Lauterbach about five days later.

* * * * * *

For as long as I had known Hein, I had heard nothing but praises for his hometown. Lauterbach was indeed a beautiful Hessian city set in rolling hills covered with farms and vineyards. It was peaceful there, and I soon began to envy Hein for having a home to return to. It didn't seem fair. The Germans living in the east had suffered the ravages of war, had been displaced from their homes, and had lost all of their belongings. The injustice of all of this seemed very profound to me. As I watched Hein being drawn into the arms of his family with tears of joy and happiness, I suddenly felt out of place. I felt as if I was intruding on

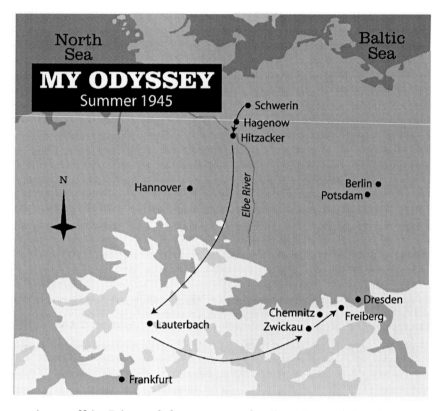

North Sea

Baltic Sea

MY ODYSSEY

Summer 1945

• Schwerin
• Hagenow
• Hitzacker

N

Hannover •

Elbe River

Berlin •
Potsdam •

• Dresden

Chemnitz •
Zwickau •

• Freiberg

• Lauterbach

• Frankfurt

a private affair. I longed for my own family; I longed for the same joyous reunion with my loved ones.

I agreed to remain in Lauterbach a few days as a guest of Hein's family, but resolved that I must get on with my Odyssey. I needed to find my way home.

Throughout our journey, Hein had told me of this wonderful municipal swimming pool in Lauterbach. We had both looked forward to a cool dip in this beautiful pool surrounded by beautiful trees and lawns. It was only a few minutes from Hein's home. So the next day we grabbed our towels and swimming suits and off we went for a swim. When we arrived, however, a sign greeted us that read:

"Off Limits to all Germans!"

I feared this was the end of our swimming adventure. We walked slowly around the pool watching American soldiers swimming, horsing around and having a good time. We noticed that at the end of the fence there was a creek that became an unfenced boundary. Hein and I decided to put our swimming trunks on and sneak in the back way to join the American soldiers. There were about 1,000 of them in the pool area, and none of them seemed interested in us. We went straight to the pool and jumped in. Several hundred American G.I.s were swimming, so I stayed low in the water and avoided coming close to any of them. The cool water was wonderful! I hadn't felt this good in a long time. I kept swimming below the water and managed to stay undetected.

After a pleasant swim, Hein and I got out and found a place to lie in the sun. There we were in the middle of hundreds of American soldiers, completely invisible, or so we thought. As I was lying in the sun, a shadow suddenly passed over me. I looked up and saw three Americans, all of whom looked like Hercules. They were talking to us, but we had no idea what they were saying. Soon they realized we were "Krauts" and became furious with us, shouting and threatening us. We gathered our belongings in silence and walked away, back to the creek. It was a close call, perhaps a foolish idea in the first place.

* * * * * * *

After a few days in Lauterbach, I decided it was time for me to head to Freiberg. I bid my new friends good-bye and started hitchhiking east to Saxony. I was able to move quickly, arriving in Zwickau, Saxony, a few days later. It was July 1945, and I noticed that I was again in an area controlled by American forces. On the east side of Zwickau, the Mulde River, a small tributary of the Elbe, separated east from west. On the other side of the Mulde, the Russians were in control. Freiberg was 50 miles farther east in the Russian zone. I was reluctant to head for Freiberg.

I knew absolutely no one in Zwickau. I was a total stranger. I did not know where to go or where I could stay. Standing in the center of the city one morning, just after I had arrived from Lauterbach, I decided I would walk through the center of town on *Bahnhof Strasse* (Train Station Street) and explore the city. I soon found a big hotel flying an American flag with several jeeps parked in front. This was the headquarters of the American Army. I was impressed and felt very comfortable with the Americans around. As I walked on farther, a sign on a door leading to a housing project suddenly caught my eye. My heart leaped into my throat as I read: "The Church of Jesus Christ of Latter-day Saints."

I was overjoyed. I had to read it several times before I could believe it. I knocked on the door and soon met a family that belonged to my church. I was so excited! They invited me in and offered me a place to stay. We talked for several hours, during which I told them my whole story. Through our conversation, I learned that several families from my hometown of Tilsit had relocated in Zwickau. I was so close to home, but I still could not bring myself to go to Freiberg.

I remained in Zwickau for several months. Each Sunday as I walked to church, I passed in front of the American headquarters. I saw the American Military Police and all the soldiers who constantly came and went from this hotel. Then, one Sunday they were gone. Unknown to me, the boundary had moved west, placing Zwickau within the Russian Zone. I had not gone to the mountain because of my dreaded fear of the Russians; now the mountain had come to me! The terribly familiar olive brown uniforms of the Russian Army, so many of which I had seen littering the landscape on the Russian Steppes, were now alive and well in Zwickau. My heart sank.

This turn of events, however, did have an upside; the last hurdle of my odyssey home was gone. It was time to find my family. With public transportation now available, the 50-mile trip to Freiberg would be easier.

* * * * * *

Late one fall afternoon in a small village outside Freiberg, my mother was working in the front yard of her small farmhouse. She looked up and saw a stranger walking toward her. As I drew closer, the rake fell from her hands. She gasped, her trembling hands covered her mouth as tears welled in her eyes. I took her into my arms and held her while we both wept uncontrollably. Never in my life had I been so happy. Never had I felt so blessed as I did standing there with my mother, holding on to dear life. I was home.

CHAPTER 17
EPILOGUE

WHEN GENERAL ALFRED JODL signed the instrument of surrender at General Eisenhower's headquarters in Rheims, France, on May 7, 1945, my days as a German soldier were officially over. However, the war did not end for me until that fall afternoon when I found my family.

Even then, some effects of the war continued. Every night my sisters had to hide in a secret place to avoid discovery by marauding Russian soldiers who regularly broke into German homes and assaulted young women. It was close to anarchy. The memory of that time still haunts many Germans who had to endure these outrages in the months and years immediately following the end of the war.

But that afternoon when I reunited with my family, with everyone except my father, the horror and losses of war were behind us. We talked all night and into the next day, giving thanks that we had survived the war. As we accounted for friends and loved ones, the reality of war became a sad endnote for people we would never see again. Faces that had disappeared, memories that would fade with time, all became very personal losses for each of us.

At the time of my reunion with my family, there was little work available for me as a former German soldier. My chances of providing support for my family decreased rapidly when I crossed into the Russian Zone. This disadvantage proved to be one of many curses that seemed to be falling on the Germans. There were no utilities and no transportation. There was only poor health care. Other services that had been common in prewar Germany were gone. One of the most critical problems that came from living in the Russian Zone was that all food went first to feed Russian soldiers. The Germans got the leftovers. We received meager rations, which turned out to be not much more than numbers on paper. There was seldom any food left for distribution among Germans. It was a particular problem in outlying rural areas, such as the village where my mother lived. So within a few days of my first visit, I returned to Zwickau where I could support myself and not be a drain on my family's meager resources.

In late 1945, there were about 6,000 Mormons living in East Germany. The German headquarters of the LDS Church were in Berlin, and in the Russian Zone the church organized into districts and branches. The church headquarters in Salt Lake City mounted a massive relief effort for its members suffering in the ruins of Europe. The church needed an infrastructure to find members and secure relief and organization for them. To help in this effort, I became a missionary in late 1945, a position that I accepted without hesitation. I had not forgotten my promise to God during the long, cold nights of my escape from Stalingrad. I relished the opportunity to serve Him by serving others in gratitude for my blessings and the blessings to my family.

As a missionary, the Russians viewed me as a "non-productive" member of society, so I received the lowest food ration available. I received stamps entitling me to a week's supply consisting of 100 grams of meat, 100 grams of margarine, 100 grams of sugar, 500 grams of potatoes or other vegetable, and 100 grams of bread. However, having stamps did not mean that we would receive food. Most of the time, shelves at food distribution centers were empty. During the bitter cold, ice and snow of the winter of 1945-46, many of us learned the true meaning of hunger, perhaps better described as famine. Germans in the cities soon resorted to begging for food from farmers and other rural suppliers.

I reported to Russian administrators at the Office of Culture and Religion. They allowed us to conduct regular church meetings, but we could not conduct any special meetings without first getting a permit. To secure a permit, we had to list the speakers and the topics of discussion. Further, the youth of the Church were expected to participate in the Young Communist organizations.

One of our first responsibilities was to organize the Relief Society, the women's organization of the Church, in the various districts and branches in East Germany. The Mormon Church has long been recognized worldwide for its welfare program, which is administered by the Relief Society. In the winter of 1945-46, church leadership was scarce. I met with groups of Mormon women who were mostly widows and living alone. So many of them were pitiful in their own right; eyes sunk deep in their sockets, their skin pale and lifeless. Yet they threw every bit of energy they had into organizing care not only for members, but for friends and neighbors as well. Their courage and devotion were an example for all of us, inspiring members to work even harder to face the hopeless conditions in which we found ourselves.

Another problem faced by the Church during the years after the war was finding a safe place to meet and minister to the needs of our members and neighbors. On one occasion, I was working in the small town of Bernburg, where an impressive castle overlooked the Saale River. The city had an upper part (*Bergstadt*) and an older, lower part (*Talstadt*). The city had not been bombed, so its beautiful Baroque buildings and Gothic churches had survived intact. But there were Russians everywhere, and I received no cooperation whatsoever from Russian administrators in trying to find facilities for the 25 or so members in that town.

One day as I was walking in the lower town, an older gentleman approached me and asked what I was doing in Bernburg. After telling him my story, I learned that this man was a Rabbi, the spiritual leader of the Jews in Bernburg. As we talked further, I learned there weren't many members of his flock left. When I told him I was looking for a suitable place for our congregation to meet, a twinkle came to his eye. He asked me to follow. Soon we came to a large open area. He explained that this was where the synagogue once stood, the only building in Bernburg that had been destroyed. As I thought about it, I guessed it had been destroyed on *Kristallnacht*, that fateful night of November 10, 1938, when synagogues were burned and Jewish businesses had been destroyed. This had been a Nazi response to the assassination in Paris of a German diplomat by the son of an exiled German Jew.

I later learned that Bernburg had been the site of even greater atrocities between November 1940 and August 1943. Here the Nazis began the systematic euthanasia of mentally ill and disabled people, and then continued with the execution of concentration camp prisoners in a gas chamber located in the basement of the Bernburg Psychiatric Hospital. Truly Satan had been abroad in this land, yet my new friend was doing everything he could to push those dark clouds away.

The Jewish community owned another building next to the open lot where the synagogue had once stood. My Rabbi friend opened the door into a large room covered with potatoes, onions and other vegetables. When he proposed that I could make good use of this room, I was speechless. His charity and kindness had exceeded anything I had ever encountered. He was so genuinely pleased to help us. In later years I have often thought of how the tragic misfortune of the Jewish community in Bernburg had been set aside by this remarkable Rabbi without a second thought, and turned unconditionally to benefit his Christian neighbors. He taught me a great lesson in love and charity, as well as the respect we must have for the variety of religious beliefs in God's Kingdom.

* * * * * *

While I was working in Bernburg, I attended a conference at the church offices in Berlin. It was winter, and the trip was difficult. In those days, the trains were running. However, the Germans rode in only the last three cars of long trains, much the same as the segregated blacks in the United States. These trains were too long, and pulled by engines fired by poor coal. Often during long trips, Russian soldiers would make their way back to the German cars and rob Germans and loot their baggage. As I returned from this meeting in Berlin to my branch in Bernburg, I was carrying a large suitcase of warm clothing that had arrived from Salt Lake City. Because this cargo was so precious, I sat with the suitcase in a dark corner under the luggage rack. As the train plodded along through the cold winter night, I heard the shouts and curses of Russian soldiers begin filtering into our car. Looking out, I saw the boots and painfully familiar olive brown uniform of a Russian soldier approaching the luggage rack above me. He was opening luggage and emptying contents onto the floor, looking for anything he might want. I hated the lawless conduct that went unchecked in this and all other trains. He hadn't seen me, but I resolved not to let him take my cargo.

As he drew near to me, I suddenly uncoiled my legs and kicked him as hard as I could in both knees. He went sprawling backwards over two seats and onto the floor, covered with bags and clothing. I leaped up, grabbed my large suitcase, tossed it off the train through an open window, and jumped after it. The deep snow made for a soft landing, but I still managed to get a few bumps and bruises. I didn't move as I watched the two red lights on the end of the train move away. Satisfied no one had decided to come after me, I gradually made my way to some lights I saw in the distance. There, sympathetic Germans took me in, and helped me continue on my way to Bernburg the next day.

Perhaps it seems odd to some that a missionary would act in this way toward another human being, but I believe that under the circumstances my behavior can be understood. For four years I had faced death at the hands of Russian soldiers who wanted to kill me and other Germans with all of their heart and soul. At this time and place, it was natural for me to fear them, to avoid them, and to despise them. It was not a season for forgiveness, at least from my perspective. My purpose under Heaven at this point in my life was to care for the people who had been placed in my stewardship. I saw that responsibility as a greater calling than giving this Russian my shirt and cloak. Still, I knew I was judging them harshly and realized that, to profess what I taught, I would need to overcome my own weaknesses. I expected that would come with time, when the time came to forgive, to build up. But that night was not a time of forgiveness for me; it was not a time when I could turn the other cheek. It was a time when it was hard to endure the tyranny of conquerors.

* * * * * * *

Two years after the end of my mission, in late 1949, I received a letter from my mother telling me that my father was alive and on his way home. By then I was married and living in Chemnitz. The news was electrifying because we had all thought him long since dead. The

Russians had captured my father in January 1945, when they overran Königsberg in East Prussia. Because he was a civilian, he was kept away from captured German soldiers and detailed to work for the Russians.

When we reunited with him in Freiberg, I was shocked. He was only a shadow of the man I once knew, a bundle of hardly anything recognizable. Here was the man who had fought tanks on the Western Front, survived imprisonment, struggled to keep our family alive and well during years of depression and famine, and now the survivor of a Russian prison. But he was alive! Our family had survived intact; bruised, but intact!

We spent long afternoons together catching up on all we had missed. So often as he would tell me his experiences, he would look out the window with eyes full of tears. His pain was overwhelming, but he had to get it out.

He would later tell me with deep emotion of the horrible atrocities he had witnessed, especially against German women. Many of these women would later take their own lives out of shame for what had happened to them. He told me of other appalling atrocities, including the sudden appearance of meat on the black market. Twenty Russian soldiers were producing it in a slaughterhouse outside Königsberg. Although it was sold as ground beef and headcheese, two German doctors known by my father, Dr. Piontek and Dr. Riwold, soon identified it for what it really was. I found it impossible to grasp the magnitude of this crime. Even though it was brought to the attention of the Russian military Commander, Lt. General D.N. Gusev, nothing ever came of the incident.

My father had worked for a time as a coachman for several Russian officers. He recalled one night when he was waiting for his officers. He was jumped by several Russian soldiers and badly beaten. Then they stole his carriage. My father managed to drag himself inside to his officers, but they seemed indifferent to the incident. They simply found another carriage and stole it from its possessors. It was a brutal, lawless time in East Prussia.

Toward the end of his captivity, Father was assigned to a Russian doctor. Each morning, he and others would accompany her through a hospital. She would identify those patients who were dead or almost so. Father was among those who were responsible for carrying these unfortunates to an open pit where they were cast in and covered with calcium oxide.

His return was a miracle, but it was not without cost. I don't think he ever really recovered from the horrible things he saw in captivity.

* * * * * *

During my years as a soldier, whether on the frozen steppes of Russia or in the summer forests of Silesia or Poland, my favorite time of day was predawn. It was a time when everything seemed quietest. It was a time when I could write letters home, when I could commune with God, when I could ponder my life and what my future might bring. On many occasions, my companion would be a beautiful Morning Star. Quite naturally, this Morning Star became a symbol of my hopes and dreams. After the end of the war, and during my service as a missionary, I began to dream of finding a companion that would spend eternity with me. I began to think of this ideal companion as my Morning Star. One day in Chemnitz, while working as a missionary, I found her.

It was inappropriate for me to have a relationship with a young woman while I was a missionary. However, when I met Traudy in Chemnitz one Sunday morning, I knew she was the one! She was busy serving as the President of all the Primary programs for small children in East Germany. She was very involved in her work and took little notice of the handsome missionaries around her. But oh, she was so very attractive! I knew she would have many eligible bachelors to choose from. My only hope was that she would still be single when I finished my mission service.

In 1947, I returned to Chemnitz. On October 25, 1947, Traudy and I were married. Our years in Chemnitz were good. I managed to find a suitable job with the *Industrieverwaltung Metallwaren*, an administrative liaison agency between the German Democratic Republic (East Germany) and 95 factories producing items made of metal.

For a few years we lived comfortably, but our dream was to emigrate to the United States, to Salt Lake City. It seemed improbable, if not impossible. But as had happened so many times before, the

Russians provided the impetus for me to move along. When I refused to join the Communist Party, my days as a salaried employee were numbered. I was branded as a politically undesirable person, and my destiny was to become a miner in the uranium-rich pitchblende mines at Aue or Schwarzenberg. I was told to report there immediately after the Easter holidays.

* * * * * * *

On Easter Sunday, 1950, we attended church and shook hands with all of our friends. Unknown to them, it would be our last time together. The following morning, Traudy and I with our young daughter Sylvia bid a tearful farewell to our family. Trying not to be conspicuous, we boarded the train for Berlin. During the four-hour trip, we had to pass through a check station manned by East German police and the KGB. My mind flashed back to the time I had encountered the Gestapo at the end of the war, and I marveled at my odyssey over the past decade. As the train slowed to a stop, another face of authority slowly made his way through the car. He inspected our papers, and asked where we were going.

"Just a short vacation with friends in Berlin."

He checked his list of undesirable people; I was not yet on it. He smiled and said, "Have a good trip." We planned to do just that.

In Berlin we arrived at the *Anhalter Bahnhof.* We passed through yet another checkpoint. Then, miraculously, we were in the American sector of Berlin being greeted by friends. We collapsed into each other's arms weeping tears of joy and gratitude. For the last time in my life, I walked away from the tyranny that sought first to destroy, then at least control my life. My ten-year Refiner's Fire was over.

A new life began for us. One of its highlights occurred almost three years later when our small family eventually settled in Salt Lake City. Here we began living the American Dream, a dream from which we would never awaken, a dream that my parents, my sister Elly, and their families would eventually share with us.

APPENDIX
FAMILY ORIGINS

IN THE EARLY 13th century, at the height of the medieval empire of Frederick II, German traders, colonists and missionaries began the first of several eastward migrations from their homeland in central Europe. Having overrun what is today eastern Germany and western Poland, the Germanic expansion spread eventually to the southeastern Baltic coast.

During roughly the same period, the Polish state of Wielkopolska, feeling the pressure of German expansion into their western territories, pushed eastward into what is now north-central Poland. Slavic White Russians, Ukranians, Lithuanians, and Borussi - or Prussians - occupied that area.[1] The Prussians, numerically inferior to the Poles, were a constant source of grief on the Polish frontier.

In 1226, after raids on the Polish settlements of Kujaway and Mazowsze, Prince Conrad of Mazowsze sent for the German Knights of the Teutonic Order to protect the Poles from marauding Prussians and Lithuanians. In return for their services, Conrad gave the Order extensive land grants, which totaled about 15,000 sq. km. in roughly the same area as today's Kaliningrad region of Russia.

The Teutonic Knights had come into existence in 1198 during the Third Crusade. Frederick Barbarossa, his red beard grayed with age, had set out with an army of 100,000 Germans in May 1189 on the Third Crusade to recapture the Holy Land and Jerusalem. After his ill-fated tumble into the Calycadnus River, about 95,000 Germans returned home, leaving their drowned emperor behind, buried at the Cathedral of Antioch. Seven years later, when civil war erupted within the Holy Roman Empire over the successor to Barbarossa's son Henry VI, most of the German soldiers remaining in the Holy Land returned to defend their homes.

A small number of knights decided to honor their vows and remain in the Holy Land, having nothing to defend back home. In his seminal work *Teutonic Knights: A Military History*, historian William Urban described the circumstances under which the order was founded:

> The soldiers from Northern Europe were not accustomed to the heat, the water or the food, and the sanitary conditions were completely unsatisfactory. Unable to bury their dead properly, they threw the bodies into the moat opposite the Accursed Tower with the rubble they were using to fill the obstacle. The stink from the corpses hung over the camp like a fog. Once taken by fever, the soldiers died like flies, their agony made worse by the innumerable insects that buzzed around them or swarmed over their bodies.[2]

By the efforts of Duke Frederick of Hohenstaufen, brother of Henry VI, and with the support of the patriarch of Jerusalem, the group received a charter from Pope Celestine III in 1198. The Order of the Hospital of St. Mary of the Germans in Jerusalem was to perform hospital services for German crusaders in the same fashion as the Knights of St. John Hospitallers, but live under the same monastic laws as the Templars.[3] They took up residence in the Gate of St. Nicholas Tower at Acre. The Teutonic Knights, as they came to be known, adopted the Templars' white robe and eight-pointed cross as their insignia, except the cross was black instead of bright red.[4] This symbol remains to this day as the familiar Iron Cross of the German Army.

When Prince Conrad sent for the Teutonic Knights in 1226, the Knights were eager to oblige. Having entered the military-monastic business much later than the Templars and Hospitallers, the Teutonic Knights had found themselves behind in the tally of pious land grants and generous endowments. The Duchy of Prussia, established by the German Knights, was given full sovereignty independent of the Holy Roman Empire, which sovereignty also extended over all lands the Knights might conquer in the future.

The Teutonic Knights assembled forces from the Holy Land and Venice and sailed down the Vistula, establishing outposts at Thorn, Culm, Elbing and Marienwerder. For the next 25 years they pushed eastward through the Baltic sands and forests, driving out many of the Prussians and Lithuanians. In 1255 they founded Königsberg, named in honor of King Ottokar of Bavaria, who had provided significant support to the Knights.

In 1309, the headquarters of the Order moved from Venice to Marienburg, on the Nogat River, which today is the city of Marbork, located in northwestern Poland. There the Knights built a magnificent castle, complete with stables, an armory, living quarters, banquet hall, and a beautiful chapel decorated with an 18-foot mosaic of the Virgin Mary.

For the next century, aspiring nobles from all over Europe dreamed of fighting under the banner of the Teutonic Knights and of gaining knighthood under the Grandmaster's sword. As the Knights secured the East Prussian frontiers, Germans moved into the duchy to repopulate areas abandoned by the retreating Slavs. Those Slavs who remained were absorbed into the Germanic community. In time, all the citizens of the duchy assumed the same name as the region's aboriginal ancestors - Prussians.

While the Knights enjoyed their Golden Age, the seeds of their own demise grew in the selfish, monopolistic commercial policies they imposed throughout the land. The profitable amber trade belonged solely to the Knights. They also controlled the grain trade, and imposed high taxes and tariffs on the Prussian traders. The suppressed Prussian merchants could not help but envy their wealthy Polish neighbors enjoying the rich markets of the Hanseatic League.[5] The harsh rule of the Knights, who rarely numbered more than 400, gradually lead to dissatisfaction and hatred of the Order. The disproportionate distribution of wealth led to widespread accusations and rumors of moral degeneration and debauchery among the Knights. The Prussians

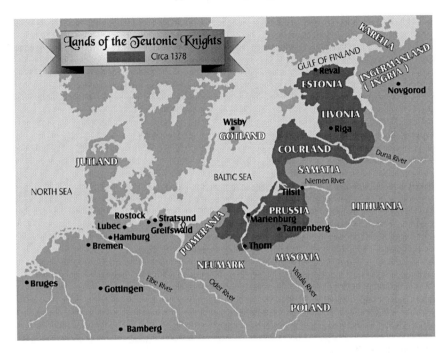

believed the Knights were more interested in wine and women than crusading the gospel among the heathen Slavs.

In 1386, Grand Prince Jagiello of Lithuania married Jadviga, who had been crowned monarch of Poland in 1384 upon the death of her father Louis I. By this marriage, Jagiello himself ascended to the throne of Poland as Vladislav II, uniting Poland with Lithuania.[6] As a result, its Slavic subjects converted *en masse* to Christianity. The event marked the beginning of the end for the Teutonic Knights, who were suddenly without a cause to crusade. Surrounded by their enemies, the Poles and Lithuanians, the Knights faced rebellion among their own Prussian subjects.

Eventually Poland declared war. In July 1410, the Knights, though fighting gallantly against impossible odds in unbearable heat, were annihilated in the Battle of Tannenberg. Thus began a century of defeats, concessions, tribute, and, finally, the complete dissolution of the Order.

After the Poles defeated the Knights in yet another war in 1519, the last Grandmaster of the Order, Albert of Hohenzollern, visited Martin Luther at Wittenberg in 1523. Luther advised the Grandmaster to abolish the Order, give up his monastic vows, take a wife and make himself the hereditary Duke of Prussia. Albert took the advice, and the Treaty of Cracow between Poland and Prussia in 1525 dissolved the Teutonic Knights. Its former grandmaster became Albert I, Duke of Prussia, a loyal vassal of the King of Poland.[7]

Albert's feebleminded son, Albert Frederick, inherited the throne in 1568. Less than a decade later he could not continue his reign without the regency of his cousin, George Frederick of Ansbach. Albert could do little more than range through manic-depressive cycles of paranoia followed by riotous dancing, drinking and debauchery. He did, however, manage to take the hand of Mary Eleanor, the eldest daughter of William the Rich of Cleves-Juelich, as his wife. It was a fortuitous marriage that had a deep impact on the future of Prussia and Europe. The Cleves-Juelich lands consisted of five duchies and counties in and near the lower Rhine. Though small, they were nonetheless the focus of an intense struggle for dominance between the Catholics, Lutherans and Calvinists in early 17th-century Europe.

The union between the feebleminded Duke and Mary Eleanor produced many children, the eldest of whom was Anna. Just before the turn of the century, daughter Anna married John Sigismund, Elector of Brandenburg, who eventually assumed his duties as regent over his mad father-in-law. The marriage united the Hohenzollern families of Prussia and Brandenburg, and cemented their claim over the pivotal Cleves-Juelich lands.[8] Most importantly, however, it eventually resulted in a grandson, Frederick William, who became the first truly gifted ruler of the Hohenzollern dynasty. The "Great Elector," as he came to be known, consolidated the Brandenburg-Prussian state, which became the powerful rival to Austria over the next century-and-a-half.

After the death in 1786 of the Great Elector's great-grandson, Frederick the Great, the Prussian state would go into a decline and eventually be humiliated by Napoleon in 1807 by the Peace of Tilsit.

* * * * * *

In the Spring of 1404, while facing mounting pressure from the united Poles and Lithuanians, the Teutonic Knights located a new fortress approximately twelve miles east of Ragnit. It was located at a strategic river crossing known as Tilsit, which linked the fertile farmlands on both sides of the Nieman River. For the next five years they fortified the position. In the disastrous campaigns of 1410-11, the fortress was heavily damaged by the Slavs, only to be rebuilt by the Knights in 1412. For the next century it served as a strategic buffer on

the Lithuanian frontier during the twilight reign of the Teutonic
Knights.

Following the Treaty of Cracow in 1525, Tilsit continued as a
geographical center of a thriving farming community and was the
strategic pivot between Catholic Lithuania and Protestant Prussia.
Gradually, a town grew around the fortress, and, under the medieval
infrastructure established by Albert I, Tilsit received a City Charter in
1552.[9]

When Calvinist John Sigismund consolidated the Hohenzollern
power over Brandenburg, Cleves-Juelich and Prussia in 1618, the
resultant Thirty Years War brought indescribable devastation to all of
Prussia. By the time the Treaty of Westphalia ended the war in 1648,
more than half of the Prussians were gone, victims of war, murder,
disease and starvation.[10] Fields laid uncultivated around the charred
ruins of hundreds of peasant villages put to the torch by marauding
mercenaries. Roads were impassable and bridges destroyed. The
economy was in ruin as counterfeiting devalued good currency. Barely
a quarter of a million Prussians survived the ordeal, and most of those
huddled within the walls of the remaining fortified cities, the fertile
farmlands having fallen into a fallow wilderness of death and desolation.

To this scene of devastation, Sigismund's grandson, Frederick
William, ascended as the Duke of Prussia in 1640. Through a series of
wise diplomatic and strategic alliances, he earned the title of the "Great
Elector." He subsequently consolidated the defenses of Prussia, laid the

foundation for a strong and efficient Prussian army, and won recognition as a sovereign in the Treaty of Oliva in 1660.[11]

By virtue of his status as a sovereign over the Duchy of Prussia, which had been granted to the Teutonic Knights independent of the Holy Roman Empire, Frederick William was an equal among the rulers of the world. However, because he was also ruler over the Brandenburg and Cleves-Juelich lands, he remained a vassal of the Holy Roman Emperor.

* * * * * * *

In 1678-79, encouraged by Louis XIV of France, the Swedes invaded Prussia again in an attempt to make territorial gains against the Great Elector. An army of 16,000 Swedish soldiers crossed the Baltic into the Memel area, occupying Tilsit into the winter. The Great Elector sent troops on sleds over the frozen fields of East Prussia and easily defeated the Swedes at the Battles of Kurisches and Frisches Haff.[11] Tilsit and the Memel area survived intact but continued to suffer from the cumulative depopulating effect of wars, invasions and famine.

As the 17th century closed, the peasant workforce in East Prussia was barely a third of what it had been when the century opened. For two years beginning in 1708, the Black Plague again decimated East Prussia's workforce. It killed almost 150,000 people, three-fourths of the population on the north side of the Nieman River.[13] Thousands of peasant farms lay vacant, and remained so until the Great Elector's grandson, Frederick William, was crowned in 1713.

Frederick William was obsessed with the miserable conditions in East Prussia and set up several programs to draw immigrants to the region. In 1727, after a bad winter, the King lamented to a close friend, " . . . the situation in Prussia is miserable. The death rate is unbelievable. If God does not give us a good year, the plague is sure to come this winter."[14] Later he wrote again, " . . . the Lord God has to give his blessing, and if he refuses to give it, that is not our fault!"[15] Shortly thereafter, King Frederick William threw in the towel and stopped granting any more funds to restore East Prussia. In 1731, however, a sudden and unexpected turn of events far to the south brought about a solution to the problem that Frederick William would forever ascribe to Divine intervention.

* * * * * * *

On October 4, 1727, to the surprise of most observers, Leopold Anton, Freiherr von Firmian was elected Archbishop of Salzburg after several ballots had failed to elect the expected favorite.[16] Firmian was an unsociable Jesuit with an undistinguished career who lacked even the support of the Emperor in Vienna and the Pope in Rome. By 1731, he had distanced himself from his own ecclesiastical court and gained a reputation as being haughty and unfriendly. In a shortsighted effort to assert his authority, Firmian decided to fire up an investigation to look into the moral and religious conditions of the Austrian regions around Salzburg.

Under the direction of the Bavarian Father Andreas Poesl, a special mission of Jesuit priests spread into the Salzach Valley and mountain districts of the Pongau to conduct house-to-house interrogations and collect the inhabitants together for hellfire and brimstone sermons. The natives were unappreciative, and particularly offended by the Jesuits' poor manners.

The Salzach River, fed by tributaries from the Pongau and Pinzgau, runs through a narrow valley that is seldom wider than a few hundred meters. Steep slopes broken by deep, wooded ravines with cascading rivers surround the valley, making it barely arable except on scattered parcels. The topography had always affected the socialization of the region. Out of necessity and practicality, it depended on small, isolated family units.

Mountain folk rarely had the opportunity to come together for broader social events, including church services. As a result, religious observation was most often conducted at a family level.

The main objects of such rituals were books, usually scriptures, and, in many cases, Protestant tracts. The latter were much more palatable to Salzburgers who had grown tired of the depressing dogma of the Catholic Church. The natural result was the replacement of Catholic ritual with more comfortable family devotions.

When Father Poesl arrived with his mission of Jesuits in the late spring of 1731, he discovered the mountain folk could easily mimic Catholics in their pious responses, but in all other mannerisms did not act like Catholics. Accordingly, the Jesuits demanded specific proof of their faith by such acts as the "angelic salutation" whereby a true believer would greet another with "Jesus Christ be praised!" to which the proper response was "in eternity." Since most social gatherings in the region were for drinking and gambling at the taverns, the locals found the greeting to border on sacrilege and refused to comply. Father Poesl returned to Salzburg, alarmed at the heresy growing in the mountains. While most Salzburgers found nothing unusual about the behavior and preferred to ignore the exaggerated warnings from the Bavarian Jesuits, Archbishop Firmian could not let it pass.

By summer, the affair had escalated into an international incident. Rather than bow to the unpopular archbishop, Salzburgers from the Pongau sought help from Protestants in Regensberg, Prussia. In July, a dubious petition became public, claiming that 19,000 Salzburgers were being oppressed by the Catholic leaders of the province. It listed several grievances.[17] The Archbishop, shocked at the magnitude of what he believed was clearly a seditious revolt, immediately sent a new commission into the Pongau. In defiance of Firmian's order not to assemble, the Salzburgers gathered at the tavern to proclaim their devotion to the Lutheran faith, to sing songs and to read scriptures. To seal their common resolve, they dipped their fingers into a box of salt and then licked them, a ritual known as *Salzlecken*.

Finally, on October 31, 1731, Archbishop Firmian issued an edict ordering the rebellious peasants out of the province. Those holding properties had until April 23, 1732 to leave. Among the 19,000 names gathered by the commission in September were the family names of Loeper and Rondek, my maternal ancestors.

* * * * * * *

On February 2, 1732, six weeks before the April departure deadline, King Frederick William of Prussia issued a formal Patent of Invitation. It stated, in part:

> In Christian-Royal mercy and heartfelt sympathy for our Evangelical coreligionist, since the aforesaid are being obliged to leave their Fatherland purely and entirely on account of their faith, We have decided to extend to them a mild and helping Hand, and to this end to receive them in Our Land, and to preserve and care for them in certain districts of our Prussian Kingdom.[18]

The Prussian proclamation requested that Archbishop Firmian treat those who desired to accept the invitation "henceforth as Prussian subjects." It ordered all German princes and towns through which the Salzburgers might travel to allow them free passage and to assist and provide care wherever possible. The Salzburg Protestants were offered free arable and meadowland, timber, and exemption from duties and

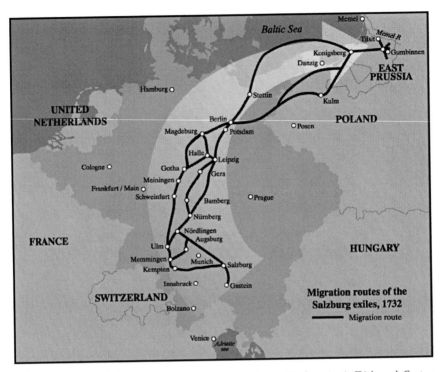

Baltic Sea

Memel

Tilsit

Memel R

Königsberg   Gumbinnen

Danzig

EAST
PRUSSIA

Hamburg

Stettin

Kulm

UNITED
NETHERLANDS

Berlin

POLAND

Magdeburg   Potsdam   Posen

Halle

Cologne   Gotha   Leipzig

Meiningen   Gera

Frankfurt / Main

Schweinfurt   Bamberg   Prague

Nürnberg

Nördlingen

FRANCE   Ulm   Augsburg

Memmingen   Munich   HUNGARY

Kempten   Salzburg

Innsbruck   Gastein

SWITZERLAND   Migration routes of the
Bolzano   Salzburg exiles, 1732
                    ——— Migration route

Venice
Adriatic sea

From Max Walker, *The Salzberg Transaction: Expulsion and Redemption in Eighteenth Century Germany*, (Ithica, NY: Cornell University Press, 1992).

fees for a period of years. They also received draft, meat and milk animals, and poultry. To further assist the immigrants, the government provided grants of tools and household goods, and seed and edible grains for the first year. As Prussian subjects, the Salzburg Protestants came under the protection of Prussia. Any harm done to them would bring reprisals from Prussia, including retaliation against the Catholic clergy in Brandenburg-Prussia.[19]

Just over a century before Brigham Young's epic exodus to Utah in 1847, my ancestors left their homes under remarkably similar circumstances. They migrated north from Austria to an unfamiliar land on a difficult and dangerous journey that cost many lives. In all, 26 columns, each of about 800 individuals, wound their way north through Nuremberg, Leipzig, Berlin, and from there to East Prussia, either direct to Königsburg by wagon or through Stettin by ship. Sixty-four trips by sea carried 10,000 Salzburgers to Königsburg on voyages during which more than 500 died, most of them children.[20] Roughly 5,000 Salzburgers made the trip overland by wagon, which claimed another 300 lives, again mostly children. Remarkably, most all the Salzburgers completed the trip between April and August of 1732. Most of them received farms already under cultivation or farms vacated by the deaths of previous owners.

The birth of my fourth great-grandparents shortly thereafter coincided with the ascension of Frederick the Great as King of Prussia in 1740. Friedrich Loeper was born in 1739 in Sternwäldchen, near Tilsit, and his future wife, Hermine Rondek, was born a year later in the same area. For the next six generations, my mother's family lived in the Tilsit area. Except for my great-grandfather, August Leopold Loeper, who was an artist, all of my Loeper ancestors were farmers. Most important, however, my maternal ancestors gave me a heritage of understanding that recognized the precepts of Martin Luther that led to the Reformation.

* * * * * * *

Naujoks[21] is a Slavic name, which has its origins in the western regions of what are today Latvia and Lithuania, south and west of Riga. My father's family was there when the Teutonic Knights arrived to establish East Prussia. It was most likely numbered among the Lithuanians who converted to Christianity *en masse* with Grand Prince Jagiello, and became Prussian when Albert I proclaimed his hereditary duchy. The Naujoks family survived the many horrendous wars and plagues. They were socialized into the strong, nationalistic heritage that found honor and duty in the service of their Prussian Fatherland, which had survived against incredible odds. Service as a Prussian soldier was never questioned; it was a duty, it was an honor, and, for many, it was a way of life.

One of the lowest points in Prussian history came in 1807 at Tilsit, when Napoleon and Czar Alexander met to divide the Prussian spoils after King Frederick William III's ignoble defeat at the hands of Napoleon the year before. Since the death of Frederick the Great in 1786, Prussia's fortunes had been on a downward slide. A low point came with the disastrous diplomacy and tactical blunders that led to the Battles of Jena and Auerstaedt on October 14, 1806. The Prussian Army was beaten decisively by Napoleon.[22]

Following the Battle of Friedland in June 1807, Russia decided to cut its losses and strike a politically expedient deal with Napoleon at the cost of its former ally, Prussia. Napoleon and Czar Alexander met for two days in seclusion on a barge in the Nieman River at Tilsit while King Frederick William and his beautiful Queen Louise cooled their heels ashore in humiliation. Even the supplications of Queen Louise on her knees before Napoleon could not prevent the partition of Prussia and the loss of its territory west and south of the Elbe River.[23] The treaty itself contained provisions that stated Prussia had no right even to exist but for the intercession of Alexander, an irony that would not be lost on the Prussians for generations to come.

The resulting occupation by French forces sparked angry voices that demanded change, kindling a new Prussian nationalism. For the first time in the eventful 19th century, concerned citizens began to look beyond the Prussian state to a German nation. Poets, philosophers, playwrights and musicians produced a panoply of works intended to promote national unity among the several German states.

King Frederick William, smarting from the humiliation at Tilsit, began to entrust more of his power to advisors. They included three Germans who were not Prussian - Baron Heinrich vom Stein from Nassau, General Neithardt von Gneisenau from Saxony, and General Gerhardt von Scharnhorst from Hanover.[24] Immediately reforms began which abolished serfdom and eliminated the rigid caste system, with its distinctions among nobles, burghers and peasants. Prussians received rights of free ownership and transfer of property, and the right to freely choose an occupation. These reforms would, according to General Gneisenau, "convert the living strength of men and the dead strength of resources into productive capital."[25]

General Scharnhorst of the Hanoverian Army, and General Gneisenau, who had served as a mercenary for the British Army in the American Revolution, both set about to reorganize the Prussian Army. Enlistments were shortened so that more men could be fully trained without exceeding the limit of 42,000 soldiers imposed by the Treaty of Tilsit. Active reserve units were established to maintain the readiness of a "Citizen's Army." The new Prussian army copied Napoleon's innovations and set up gymnastic societies to strengthen the physical and moral development of Prussian youth.

By 1810, war between France and Russia was inevitable. Though Prussia had secretly suggested an alliance with Russia, Czar Alexander declined and chose instead to wage a defensive battle. Without Russian backing, King Frederick William had no choice but to agree to Napoleon's demand for 10,000 troops to fight in Russia. However, on December 30, 1812, General Hans von Yorck, without consent from the King, defected to the side of the Russians and placed his army in East Prussia to defend the Russian right flank.[26] General von Yorck agonized over violating his oath of loyalty, and rationalized that Prussian people wanted war against Napoleon. The King, however, was not free to heed the needs of his nation, so, accordingly, General von Yorck believed he was justified in his actions. General von Yorck based his flagrant violation of his oath of allegiance on a conviction that it was the only chance Prussia would have to regain its honor.

In the annals of Prussian military history, he would become, for generations to come, a symbol of justifiable insubordination that would one day motivate a well-organized attempt on Hitler's life at his headquarters in East Prussia. The Kreisau Circle, as the conspiracy was known, included descendants of several noble Prussian families, including Count Helmut von Moltke and Count Peter Yorck von Wartenburg.

General von Yorck's gamble paid off, and within a year Napoleon left to his first exile. After Napoleon's final defeat at Waterloo and the Second Peace of Paris in 1815, the stage was set for the unification of German states into the Second Reich. This unification would ultimately take place a half-century later.[27] At the same time, diplomatic agreements and alliances arose that one day would position all the European powers into a disastrous puzzle that would result in two major world wars.

* * * * * * *

In August of 1871, as General Moltke watched his Krupp cannons annihilate the beautiful red and blue turbaned French Zouaves at Sedan, my great-grandfather, George Naujoks, a soldier of the Prussian cavalry, waited quietly on his horse. Before his eyes a harbinger of the future boomed across what had once been a free maneuvering zone for cavalry and infantry platoons. The Kruppstahl cannons from the Ruhr Valley had stretched the long arm of death even farther, as war became a pure science of killing. The glorious charge of cavalry and orderly maneuver of infantry platoons became obsolete as battles would now be won or lost by focusing artillery fire on grid positions as impersonal as a chessboard.

The war was over quickly, but its impact on my family's future was lasting. With a unified Germany, Prussian pride ran deep. My grandfather, George Naujoks, would tell the story of his father in the Franco-Prussian war many times. My grandfather also spoke often and with pride of his own service in the Prussian cavalry, recounting his greatest experience as the day he passed in review before the Kaiser himself. My vague recollections of grandfather include boots polished like mirrors and the archetypal curl of a Prussian mustache. It did not take much for me to imagine his stern, rugged face under a gleaming black and gold Pickelhaube. Though his strength and stature may have seemed imposing to a casual observer, I knew him much better as a warm and loving patriarch. He would eventually die a few weeks after his 80th birthday, on September 17, 1944, shortly before the Russian army crossed the Memel River into East Prussia. To this day, the circumstances of grandfather's death remain a mystery; but given the situation at that time, I can only imagine the tragedy he faced at the end of his life.

* * * * * *

The morning of St. John's Eve, June 23, 1917, was unusually quiet on the German front line between Arras and Cambrai in northeast France. My 22-year old father, Oscar Naujoks, stood guard as a sentry on the early morning watch while his comrades slept soundly in their well-fortified bunkers. As he sat quietly with his helmet off enjoying the cool dawn breeze, he gazed west over the barren and scarred no man's land that separated him from the enemy, as it had for the last several months. Concertina wire and barren tree stumps littered the landscape. Numerous deep craters from innumerable artillery barrages, were filled with stagnant water, decomposing warriors, and traces of many poisons that had found a new and deadly use in the progress of human warfare.

The war had been going for almost three years, and now the Americans were joining the fight. The strategic outlook for Germany was not good. My father could not grasp what the distant future held for him. He lived from day to day, wondering if each dawn would be his last. As he later reflected, this day came the closest to being his last.

Just before he was due to be relieved at his post, the British artillery opened up and began ranging toward the German lines. In the din of explosions, a new and confusing noise echoed across the battlefield. It sounded as if hundreds of trucks were heading in his direction, which seemed absurd because of the impassable moonscape between the German and British lines.

Gradually the noise grew louder as the artillery barrage faded off. My father peered over the top of the trench and was stunned by an amazing sight - armored vehicles rolling up and down the battlefield, sometimes disappearing completely into the craters. It seemed as if there were hundreds of steel monsters rolling toward German lines, followed closely by British infantry.

The German artillery commenced firing immediately as sleepy soldiers stumbled out of the bunkers into the trench, dazed by the confusing sight before them. Suddenly a wave of khaki poured over the top of the trench accompanied by unfamiliar foreign shouts. My father was on his back in the trench as hundreds of British Tommies poured over the German position. Time suddenly stood still as my father gazed up into the eyes of a British soldier whose bayonet was pressing hard against his chest. Slowly my father raised his arms in a gesture of surrender, expecting that his next breath would probably be his last. A sudden kick in the behind and profuse English cursing broke the tension. Miraculously, my father was taken prisoner with several others from his unit. For him, the war was over.

Capture was most certainly a blessing that preserved him from the horrible fighting that would take place on the Western Front over the next 18 months. Imprisoned near Calais, my father was finally released in 1919 to return to a Germany without its Kaiser and in total economic collapse. For my father, however, nothing could take away the joy he felt returning to East Prussia.

The sting of defeat and the adhesive and confusing terms of The Treaty of Versailles hung over East Prussia like a Sword of Damocles. Nonetheless, happy to be alive and home with his family, my father returned to farming on a small plot north of the Memel River. As time passed, he came to know a beautiful young Prussian woman, Ida Loeper, whose family had arrived in East Prussia almost two centuries earlier, during the 1732 migration from Salzburg. In uncertain times and looking to a future without promise, they married in April 1920. The Protestant heritage of my mother's family united with the proud Prussian traditions of my father. This marriage created a family of loyalty, tolerance and love that would markedly affect my young life in the next two decades, through seemingly impossible circumstances and against incredible odds.

Author's Note

FIRST AND FOREMOST, this book is a memoir, the recollections of someone who experienced some of the most intense and frightening events in human history. Art Naujoks' experiences were not unique, but his perspective was. As a German member of The Church of Jesus Christ of Latter-day Saints, he embraced beliefs and doctrines that required his allegiance to the rulers of his nation, even though he was reluctant to give that allegiance. Though the doctrine was black and white, its application, from his viewpoint, fell into various shades of gray with regard to his experiences as a youth in the church and as a soldier on the Eastern Front between 1942 and 1945.

In writing this book, we did not intend to create a detailed historical analysis of the events described herein. Our purpose was to recount these events within a general historical context that might possibly provide the reader with a better understanding of our subjective viewpoint. Accordingly, several secondary sources have been cited in the creation of this manuscript. Some readers may take exception to the historical works we cite, while others may disagree with the context and generalizations adopted in the text. For this potential offense, we apologize in advance, and defer a more critical analysis to those experts who have provided the world with almost inexhaustible scholarship, which far exceeds the scope of this work. Any errors in our analysis, of which there may be many, are purely unintentional; nonetheless, we accept sole responsibility for them.

The fundamental source of this book is an unpublished manuscript written by Arthur O. Naujoks, Jr. in 1989 entitled *From the Trenches of Stalingrad to the Rocky Mountains*. It was written at a momentous time for German people all over the world. The Berlin Wall was coming down, and reunification was certain. Events that had haunted many Germans for over four decades were coming to closure, and so it was for Art Naujoks. He had gathered his recollections over a lifetime, assembling them in that manuscript for posterity.

By 1989, Art had long since become an American citizen. As the remarkable events in Eastern Europe unfolded, he felt that he could finally speak more openly of his experiences. He never stopped expressing to the world how grateful he was for the many blessings he believed he had received in the aftermath of such horrific events long ago in a place so distant in time and memory. He often commented how remarkable it was to eventually be leading a new life of prosperity in America. It was a land which, on one hand, was the center of the universe for his religion but, on the other, populated by people who were at one time his enemy. His neighbors were people, who, under certain circumstances, would have readily taken his life.

Those who knew Art understood clearly that he was proud to be an American. Only those closest to him, his family and close friends, ever knew of his remarkable past. Art Naujoks was a humble man, and the text of his manuscript reflects it. For instance, nowhere in the nearly 270 pages of hand-typed manuscript is there any mention of his award of the Iron Cross Second Class. Those familiar with the Iron Cross will know that, generally speaking, it is an award that gets progressively higher for repetitive acts of valor. His award came in September 1942 when, in the face of an attack by seemingly overwhelming Russian forces, he stood his ground while those around him fled. Hauptmann von Langenstein, his much-admired senior officer, witnessed his bravery and rallied the troops to stop the attack. Thereafter, several other acts of heroism described here (which Art always discounted as routine) certainly warranted higher awards. Unfortunately, few if any senior officers ever survived to make such recommendations. To be sure, medals for heroism were never foremost in Art's mind as he fought desperately to survive in situations where the chances of survival were low.

Art and I met often over seven years to discuss many subjects in his manuscript. He often wrote a page or two about events that I subsequently expanded into a chapter. To do that, I often wrote long lists of questions to flesh out certain facts or to get a better understanding of what he was thinking. After I revised several pages of text, Art reviewed them, making corrections and comments. Many times I provided a broad-brush of historical background culled from extensive reading I had undertaken to understand the strategic implications of his tactical experiences. More often than not, he corrected my errors and then enlightened me with an overwhelming amount of information.

Art's favorite book on Stalingrad was William Craig's *Die Schlacht um Stalingrad: Der Untergang der 6. Armee Kriegswende an der Wolga,* The German version of Craig's popular work, *Enemy at the Gate.* I relied on Anthony Beevor's excellent account in *Stalingrad: The Fateful Siege: 1942-1943* and V.E. Tarrant's *Stalingrad: Anatomy of an Agony.* These works I supplemented with several other books, but few, if any, mentioned the plight of Axis soldiers surrounded on the Don Bend in December 1942. It was not until December 2002 that I was able to obtain several accounts of Italian soldiers trapped near the Don Bend and the remarkable memoir of Guy Sajer, *The Forgotten Soldier. (See* footnote 5 to Chapter 11).

As a general road map through German history, I used an old college text, John Rodes' *Germany: A History,* which was helpful for understanding the administration of postwar Germany. My copy of Dr. Rodes' text was published in 1964 at the height of the Cold War, and thus reflected a Western interpretation commensurate with the time.

Of particular interest was *The Salzburg Transaction: Expulsion and Redemption in Eighteenth-Century Germany* by Mack Walker, which describes in detail a unique historical exodus that is remarkably similar to the Mormon migration to Utah in 1847. Art's Austrian ancestry was a matter of particular pride for him, and this historical likeness to the Mormon pioneers gave him some degree of pleasure when he discussed it with his Utah neighbors.

Another book that was particularly useful was Gertrude Mackprang Baer's *In the Shadow of Silence: From Hitler Youth to Allied Internment: A Young Woman's Story of Truth and Denial*, which I picked up in Toronto in early October 2002.

Dr. Baer's commentary on the Third Reich's social, political and racial structures provides valuable insight into an entire generation of Germans, a generation which included Art Naujoks. It is a generation that does not seek to avoid its involvement in a dark chapter of German history, but instead searches for understanding. A search for the explanation for what Dr. Baer described as "a fatal combination of Führer idolatry, political naïveté, personal cowardice, deference to authority, and - most pertinent of all - societal distrust of non-German blood, culture and tradition" (Baer, p. 180-181).

Art expressed, in so many words, a desire to find closure with Germany's past. But he disdained the emotional panegyrics of revisionist historians who seemed to demand proof for the nonexistence of a thesis as a means of proving the correctness of their thesis. "It sounds too much like Nazi physics," he once chuckled in one of our meetings, referring to a term often used by historians to describe the moronic attempt of the Nazis to ignore the Jewish contribution to atomic physics.

To be sure, Art was not happy with Daniel Goldhagen's *Hitler's Willing Executioners* and its conclusion that the vast majority of Germans would have willingly participated in the execution of Jews. Through Dr.

Baer's clearly expressed and understandable analysis, he found a kindred spirit. Dr. Baer gently rejects young Goldhagen's subjective thesis as impossible to substantiate, and points out the term of collective guilt is "no longer a question of historical truth, but merely one of semantics" (Baer, p. 180).

Contributing further to this understanding is Richard Rhodes' powerful analysis in *Masters of Death: The SS-Einsatzgruppen and the Invention of the Holocaust*. Although he does agree that ideology may be used to justify violent behavior, Rhodes rejects Goldhagen's eliminationist anti-Semitism theory which suggests that most Germans believed "...Jewish influence, by nature destructive, must be eliminated irrevocably from society." Rhodes points out that Goldhagen's theory, and the idea that "people must be motivated to kill others, or else they would not do so," as naïve and tautological. It fails to explain the Nazi obsession with murdering not only the Jews, but the Slavs, Gypsies, homosexuals and the disabled (Rhodes, p. 20-21).

Using the far more empirical work of Lonnie Athens, Rhodes analyzes the inception of the Holocaust in the brutal activities of the SS-Einsatzgruppen who followed the Wehrmacht into the Soviet Union beginning in June 1941. With analysis that goes beyond the normative conjecture of Goldhagen, Rhodes points out that:

> ...motivation is not sufficient by itself to produce serious violence; people must also have undergone prior violent experiences: they must have *learned* to be violent and must have come to identify themselves as violent.

Otherwise their intense hatreds will emerge as ugly but nonviolent behaviors, such as expressions of contempt, denunciations, discrimination, ostracism - exactly the sort of behaviors that the rest of twentieth century Europe, and Germany before Hitler, demonstrated towards the Jews. As several critics have noted, Goldhagen's theory that eliminationist anti-Semitism explains the Holocaust also isolates the most destructive genocide of the twentieth century as a unique event (in Goldhagen's formulation, "a radical break with everything known in human history"), disconnected from the other genocides of the age, when in fact other genocides - of the Armenians, for example, or of the Tutsi in Rwanda - resembles the Holocaust in etiology if not in scale even though anti-Semitism played no part in their occurrence (Rhodes, p. 21).

Art often wondered how it was that Josef Stalin's mass genocide of the Soviet collectivization period escaped the scrutiny and condemnation of Americans. For strategic reasons, perhaps the misdeeds of an ally can be overlooked by the historians of the victors – a sad realization for many of the vanquished, especially when they are accused *en masse* of eliminationist anti-Semitism.

There have been two developments in Mormon historiography as it relates to World War II that are relevant to this memoir. First is the continuing discussion and analysis through publications and media of the Helmuth Hübener Group. To be sure, Helmuth Hübener's heroic but tragic resistance to the Third Reich is a defining moment for German Mormons. Its significance, however, poses some difficulty for Germans who disagreed with Helmuth's particular course of action but were nonetheless decidedly anti-Nazi. The three days of intensive interrogation of Helmuth's branch president in 1942 and the subsequent warning from the Gestapo that "You Mormons are next" typifies the multifaceted problem faced by many German Mormons. On one hand, Church members are quick to embrace the heroism and martyrdom of Helmuth at the hands of the Nazis. However, for those living in 1942, taking a similar position could have been fatal.

I remember how incensed I was in the late 1970s when, as a law student at BYU, I learned that Helmuth had been excommunicated for resisting Hitler. Over the years since, I have come to understand that Helmuth's branch president worked frantically to protect his branch members from being dragged into the conspiracy. After years of exhaustive discussion, the ire of my youth has given way to a realization that I had judged too quickly and too passionately. It now appears the excommunication was procedurally flawed, which to me suggests that it was undertaken to appease the Gestapo more than to discipline Helmuth.

Art and I had many conversations about the Hübener Group. Karl-Heinz Schnibbe has stated that he does not fault anyone for either supporting or disdaining his participation in the Hübener Group. We also agreed that a non-judgmental approach to Helmuth's actions was both prudent and appropriate. This also follows for other acts of individual resistance adopted by many Church members, some of which have come to light over the years and others that remain private and personal to German members to this day.

A second development in more recent years has been the establishment of the Saints at War project at Brigham Young University. This book is published in support of that project. We have written this with the hope that it provides a useful contribution to understanding the myriad experiences of church members who took part in the various wars for various causes in our collective lifetimes.

I also acknowledge the impact of the Internet on historical research. While most anything can be found on the Internet if one searches long enough, it is nonetheless a repository of remarkable documents and sources. Internet research can provide the means to corroborate data already in hand and find additional supporting material. My research for this book was significantly enhanced by use of the Internet. In most cases, I found summaries of material that led me to specific books and articles in local public and university libraries. In other instances, I found authoritative articles that were otherwise unavailable. As time goes by, I expect the Internet will expand, with even greater capabilities, a continuing development I eagerly anticipate each time I log on. Suffice it to say, however, that this book was improved substantially by the use of broader, more open communications among a variety of scholars and repositories throughout the world. These communications were significantly facilitated by the Internet.

I should point out the greatest authority on this memoir is now silent. Art died peacefully on Friday evening, October 25, 2002 while listening to his favorite German music in his study at home. It was his 55th wedding anniversary. Having known Traudy, his lovely wife who passed away a few years ago, I have no doubt of the circumstances of this much-deserved, peaceful passing. I miss him terribly and treasure the many years of friendship that I enjoyed with Art. I enjoyed not only the preparation of this memoir but also sharing his many anecdotes and insights into a multitude of subjects, both historical and contemporary.

Finally, I want to acknowledge the assistance of many friends and colleagues whose input has been responsible for my completing this project. First, I am extremely grateful to Joel Izatt for the graphic design of maps and the cover, and for touching up the photographs from Art's album. LDS readers are familiar with Joel's work from his original design of the CTR symbol in the late 1950s. Along with Joel, I could not have finished this book without the help of Ray Cornia, who did the layout, and helped with suggestions and comments. Ray has the unique ability to make a good book great, and I will be forever indebted to him.

I would like to thank Dean Hughes for his words of advice. I am grateful for his sage wisdom, but more appreciative of his friendship. My cousin Lorainne Quillon edited the manuscript after an initial read by several friends and family members, including my parents, Wayne and Bonnie Eldredge and big brother Dave, my good friends Sherrie Craig, McKay Daines, Pam Blevins, Bill Weiss, Cory Maxwell at Deseret Book and others who provided brief and insightful comments.

Special thanks go to Mario Naujoks who supported his father's efforts and continues to see his many projects through to completion.

I am also grateful to my children, Russ, Nate, Monica, Crissy, Nichole, Joe, Mikey and Sophie who over the years have endured my many expressions of exasperation, tantrums when the computer crashed, and other inconveniences suffered when there is a writer in the house.

I owe a debt of gratitude to my parents, Wayne and Bonnie Eldredge; one that can never be repaid. Your unconditional love has been a blessing throughout my life. You'll never know how appreciated and loved you have been every day of my existence. Thank you from the bottom of my heart.

Last but not least, my love and appreciation to my wife Michelle for not strangling me in my sleep when she had many good opportunities and reasons. She was my coach, my critic, my support and encouragement, and in the end, the one who wanted most to see this in print. Words can never express how much I cherish you.

Michael S. Eldredge
Salt Lake City, Utah
Memorial Day
May 31, 2004

REFERENCES

Chapter I - Surrounded

[1]German lyrics to *Silent Night, Holy Night*:

Stille Nacht, Hielige Nacht
Alles schlaft, einsam wacht.
nur das traute hoch heilige Paar.
Holder Knabe im lockigen Haar
Schlaf in himmlischer Ruh,
Schlaf in himmlischer Ruh!

Joseph Mohr, *Stille Nacht, Hielige Nacht*, ed. Marianne Mehling. *Frohe Weihnacht: Geschichten, Lieder und Gedichte zur Advents und Weihnachtszeit,* (Munich: Droemer-Knaur, 1986) 233.

[2]At Stalingrad, I was a member of Battery 9 of the Heavy Artillery Battalion, 376th Artillery Regiment, 376th Infantry Division, 8th Army Corps, German 6th Army.

[3]Carl von Clausewitz, *On War,* (New York: Penguin Classics, 1982) 102.

[4]*Ibid.,* 103.

Chapter II - A Youth in East Prussia

[1]Rodes, *Germany: A History,* 489.

[2]Piers Brendon, *The Dark Valley: A Panorama of the 1930s,* (New York: Alfred A. Knopf, 2000) 31-34.

[3]Karl May was the German author of a multi-volume set of adventure books about the American West set in the mid-nineteenth century featuring such characters as the Indian Chief Winnetou and Old Shatterhand. The series was especially popular among German youth in the early 1900s but fell out of favor after the Nazis came to power.

[4]Yves Bonnefoy, *Dictionnaire des Mythologies et des religions des Sociétiés Traditionnelles et du Monde Antique*, (Paris: Centre National des Lettres, 1981) trans. Wendy Doniger, as *American, African and Old European Mythologies*, (Chicago: University of Chicago Press, 1993) 251.

[5] *Ibid.*, 251-252. *See also* Barry Cunliff, ed., *The Oxford Illustrated Prehistory of Europe*, (Oxford: Oxford University Press, 1994) 321.

[6]Joseph Campbell, *The Mythic Image*, (Princeton, NJ: Princeton University Press, 1974) 34. *See also* Norman Davies, *Europe: A History*, (New York: HarperCollins Publishers, Inc., 1998) 280-281.

Chapter III - Come the Saints

[1]National Socialist German Workers' Party. For an excellent analysis of German attitudes toward National Socialism, *see* Gertrude Mackprang Baer, *In the Shadow of Silence: From Hitler Youth to Allied Internment: A Young Woman's Story of Truth and Denial*, (Toronto: Harper Collins Publishers, Ltd. 2002).

[2]There is some question among historians as to whether or not members of the Church of Jesus Christ of Latter-day Saints were singled out as targets of Nazi bigotry. Given the doctrine requiring Mormons to be loyal citizens of the land in which they live, it seems logical that Mormons would not have been looked upon in any manner differently than German Catholics or Protestants. It can be said that Hitler hated all religions because they posed a threat to his totalitarian control of the country, and that he, in fact, was attempting to acquire the same reverence from his people as they were devoting in their religious

worship. One contrasting example is the persecution of the Christians who were Jehovah's Witnesses. At the time Hitler came to power, there were about 25,000 Jehovah's Witnesses in Germany. Central to their core beliefs was the rejection of secular authority and an expressed refusal to salute Hitler, vote in elections or bear arms for Germany, almost the polar opposite of Mormon beliefs. Jehovah's Witness congregations were subject to harassment, meetings were disrupted and members were beaten and arrested. In spite of their attempts to convince Hitler that they were politically "neutral," the Jehovah's Witnesses were banned on April 1,1935. By the end of the war, over 10,000 members had been sent to concentration camps where as many as 6,000 died, at least 300 of them by execution. Jehovah's Witnesses were given the opportunity to avoid imprisonment by simply renouncing their religious doctrine. The vast majority refused, and earned their place in concentration camps with a distinct purple triangle sewn on their clothing.

The LDS Church did not suffer the same harassment as the Jehovah's Witnesses; it was not targeted by a similar organized Nazi campaign of persecution. Yet, as Art points out in his encounter with Herr Karcher in Heilsburg in 1943-1944 (Chapter XII), Mormon attitudes and beliefs towards Jews would certainly have run foul of Nazi doctrine.

It is important to note that the resistance by Jehovah's Witnesses to the Nazis was not so much specific, as it was a general rejection of all world governments. It is also significant that Jehovah's Witnesses were not so much pacifists as they were soldiers in God's Kingdom, which is not of this world. These beliefs were, and are, doctrinal distinctions that separate Jehovah's Witnesses from the vast majority of all other Christian churches and doctrines, including the LDS Church.

Hitler overcame his ideological conflict with Christianity on two broad fronts. First, he quietly eliminated his strongest religious-based political adversary in Germany, the Catholic Center Party, in a controversial treaty signed in the early summer of 1933. Much to the consternation of German Catholics, the Nazis agreed to the Reich Concordat negotiated by the Vatican Secretary of State, Cardinal Eugenio Pacelli, who would later become Pius XII. Briefly, Hitler guaranteed the right of the Catholic Church to independently regulate its ecclesiastical affairs in Germany in exchange for the Church's agreement to stay out of secular matters under the control of the German government. Almost overnight, the political party disbanded, auxiliary organizations ceased to exist, and a muffle was placed on activists in the clergy who were outspoken over Hitler's bullying tactics. For Rome, it was the sovereign recognition the Church needed, but it was paid for at an enormous price. For an excellent analysis of the Reich Concordat, see John Cornwell, *Hitler's Pope: The Secret History of Pius XII,* New York: Penguin Putnam, Inc., 1999.

Where the Catholic Church had presented a single united front, easily handled by the concordat, there were, at the same time, 45 million German Protestants that belonged to twenty-eight Lutheran and Reformed Churches. The largest of these was the Church of the Old Prussian Union. Hitler's main strategy was to find a means of unifying them under one authority, and then striking the same type of agreement whereby the Protestants would not interfere with the ruling Nazis. This process took longer, and extended into the period of increasing persecution of Jews, which drew strong protest on many Protestant fronts. Hitler's chief opposition came from Rev. Martin Niemöller, a fearless and popular minister of the Church of Jesus Christ located in Dahlem, an affluent suburb of Berlin. Niemöller was a former WWI U-boat skipper who at first applauded Hitler's rise to power, but then turned against the Nazi regime. He effectively led Protestant opposition against the Nazis and their puppet German Christian Faith Movement, which embraced the regime's anti-Semitism and saw little use for the Old Testament. By 1937, however, Hitler had installed a new Minister for Church Affairs, Dr. Hans Kerrl, who slowly tightened the Nazi grip over defiant Protestant ministers. Niemöller was arrested and tried by the same court that would eventually convict Helmut Hübener. Because Niemöller had preached in public, he was acquitted of attacks against the state, but he soon found himself in protective custody, eventually at Sachsenhausen and Dachau, from where he was liberated in 1945. For an excellent discussion of Hitler's struggle with the Protestants of Germany, see William Shirer, *The Nightmare Years 1930-1940: A Memoir of a Life and the Times.* (Boston: Little, Brown and Company, 1984).

During the Helmuth Hübener investigation, when Gestapo agents interrogated branch president Arnold Zöllner, himself a member of the Nazi Party, he was reportedly told upon release that after the Jewish issue was finished, the Mormons would be next. In considering this statement within the total context of Hitler's policy towards Christians and their churches, except for the active persecution of Jehovah's Witnesses, it appears that comment was more likely intended to be a stern warning or scare tactic than a hint of an organized campaign of persecution aimed at Mormons looming on the horizon.

- MSE

[3]J. Remak, ed., *The Nazi Years: A Documentary History*, (Englewood Cliffs, NJ: Prentice-Hall, 1969) 57-58.

[4]H.W. Koch, *The Hitler Youth: Origins and Development 1922-1945*, (New York: Barnes & Noble Books, 1975) 115. *See also,* Marcus Wendel, *Third Reich Fact Book*, accessed 14 May 2001, available from http://www.skalman.nu/third-reich

[5]For a complete and authoritative account of the Helmuth Hübener Group, *see* Blair R. Holmes and Alan F. Keele, *When Truth was Treason: German Youth Against Hitler*, (Urbana, IL: University of Illinois Press, 1995). *See also* Karl-Heinz Schnibbe, *The Price: The True Story of a Mormon Who Defied Hitler*, (Salt Lake City, UT: Bookcraft, Inc., 1984), Rudi Wobbe and Jerry Borrowman, *Three Against Hitler*, (Salt Lake City: Covenant Communications, Inc., 1996); and Rick McFarland and Matt

Whitaker, *Truth and Conviction*, (Provo, UT: Brigham Young University, 2002) DVD Documentary Video.

Chapter IV - Storm Clouds

[1]David McCullough, *Truman*, (New York: Simon & Schuster, 1992) 266-267.

[2]Joseph H. Field, "Fischer-Tropsch Process" in Sybil P. Parker, ed., *The McGraw-Hill Concise Encyclopedia of Science and Technology, 2nd Edition*, (New York: McGraw-Hill Publishing Company, 1989) 775.

[3]"The Integration of the German Oil, Chemical, Rubber and Explosives Industries," in *The U.S. Strategic Bombing Survey: European Theater of Operations, 2nd Edition*, (Washington, D.C.: Government Printing Office, 1947) accessed 14 September 2002, available from http://www.members.tripod.com/~Sturmvogel/ussbint.html

[4]"The How and Why Air Attacks Crippled the German Oil-Chemical Industry: Synthetic Oil Targets," in *The U.S. Strategic Bombing Survey: European Theater of Operations, 2nd Edition*, (Washington, D.C.: Government Printing Office, 1947) accessed 14 September 2002, available from http://members.tripod.com/~Sturmvogel/ussbssyn.html

[5]Holmes and Keele, *When Truth was Treason*, 30. *See also* Schnibbe, *The Price*, 25.

[6]Holmes and Keele, *When Truth was Treason*, 70-71.

[7]Brendon, *The Dark Valley*, 534-538.

[8]Henry Kissinger, *Diplomacy*, (New York: Simon & Schuster, 1994) 310-316.

Chapter V - A Soldier of the Reich

[1]Daniel W. Michaels, "New Evidence on the 1941 'Barbarossa' Attack: Why Hitler Attacked Soviet Russia When He Did," *Journal of Historical Review,* 18 No.3 (May/June 1999) 40, reviewing Adolph von Thadden, *Stalins Falle: Er Wollte den Kreig,* (Rosenheim, DE: Kultur und Zeitgeschicte/Archiv der Zeit, 1996). accessed 14 September 2002, available from http://www.ihr.org/ jhr/v18n3p40_Michaels.html

[2]Alexander Werth, *Russia at War 1941-45,* (Carroll & Graf Publishers, Inc., 1964) 132-143.

[3]Michaels, "New Evidence," *Journal of Historical Review,* 40-43. General Vlassov is discussed further in Chapter IX *infra. See* endnote 11, Chapter IX - Eastern Front.

Chapter VI - France

[1]Kissinger, *Diplomacy,* 267-69.

[2]Brendon, *The Dark Valley,* 160-162.

[3]E. Turner, "The Phony War," in I.C.B. Dear, ed., *The Oxford Companion to World War II,* (Oxford: Oxford University Press, 1995) 885-887.

[4]Matthew Cooper, *The German Army 1933-1945,* (Lanham, MD: Scarborough House, 1978) 232-236.

[5]Roderick Kedward, "France," in Dear, *The Oxford Companion to World War II,* 396-408.

[6]Dear, "Baedeker Raids" in *The Oxford Companion to World War II,* 101.

[7]The first 1,000 RAF bomber raid sorties against Cologne in May 1942. *See* Dear, "Bombers", in *The Oxford Companion to World War II*, 147.

Chapter VII - Operation Blue

[1]Antony Beevor, *Stalingrad: The Fateful Seige: 1942-1943*, (New York: Penguin Books, 1999) 70.

[2]Cooper, *The German Army*, 309, 328.

[3]General Heinz Guderin, *Panzer Leader*, (Cambridge, MA: Da Capo Press, 1996) 219.

[4]Werth, *Russia at War*, 205.

Chapter VIII - Eastern Front

[1]Werth, *Russia at War*, 443.

[2]V.E. Tarrant, *Stalingrad: Anatomy of an Agony*, (London: Leo Cooper, 1992) 40.

[3]Werth, *Russia at War*, 415-416.

[4]*Ibid. See also:* James Lucas, *War on the Eastern Front: The German Soldier in Russia, 1941-1945,* (reprint, London: Greenhill Books, 1998) 55-59.

[5]Tarrant, *Stalingrad*, 38.

[6]*Ibid.*

[7]Richard Overy, *Russia's War: A History of Russia's War Effort: 1941-1945*, (New York: Penguin Books, 1998) 161-163.

[8]Werth, *Russia at War*, 410-414.

[9] Alexei Surkov, "I Hate", published in *Red Star*, August 12 1942, quoted in Werth, *Russia at War*, 413.

[10]Ilya Ehrenburg, published in *Red Star*, August 13 1942, quoted in Werth, *Russia at War*, 414.

[11] Lieutenant General Andrei Vlassov was the Commander of the Russian Second Shock Army when he was captured by the Germans in July 1942, after Moscow failed to give him necessary support and his troops were surrounded. Vlassov was facing certain punishment by the Russians for ordering his troops to disburse in the face of the High Command's order not to retreat, so he basically had nothing to lose working for the Germans. Sensing a possible opportunity for himself in what appeared to be certain victory for the Germans, Vlassov agreed to organize an anti-Stalinist Russian Liberation Movement from captured officers and soldiers of the Red Army. He quickly became embroiled in political intrigue that was far over his head. Subsequently captured by American troops, he was turned over to the Red Army, which hanged him on August 1, 1946. *See* John Erickson, *The Road to Berlin: Stalin's War with Germany*, (New Haven: Yale University Press, 1999) 93-94.

Chapter IX - Home Again

[1]Beevor, *Stalingrad*, 239-251.

[2]Overy, *Russia's War*, 179.

[3]Werth, *Russia at War*, 501-507.

Chapter X - Retreat

[1]Erickson, *The Road to Berlin*, 46-49.

[2]Major General F.W. von Mellenthen, *Panzer Battles: A study of the Employment of Armor in the Second World War*, (Norman, OK: University of Oklahoma Press, 1956) 252.

[3]James Lucas, *Das Reich: The Military Role of the 2nd SS Division*, (Reading, Berks.: Cassell Military Paperbacks, 1999) 92-97.

[4]John Pimlott, *The Historical Atlas of World War II*, (New York: Henry Holt and Company, 1995) 120-121.

[5]In addition to the German soldiers trapped behind the Russian encirclement, thousands of Hungarian and Italian troops entrenched north of the 9th Battery *B-Stelle* on the west side of the Don River were trapped as well. Several accounts were written by other soldiers in similar situations described by Mr. Naujoks herein; however, in most instances, these accounts involve soldiers who were either not encircled, or managed to escape in a shorter period of time south and west of Sudzah. One German soldier's account was written by Guy Sajer, who was a French conscript first attached to a German supply unit as a driver, and later assigned as a *landser* or infantry soldier, attached to the *Gross Deutschland* Division. His account of the Eastern Front parallels many of the descriptions herein that are relatively near to the same locations described by Mr. Naujoks. Sager's account is widely regarded as the classic and most descriptive memoir of a German soldier on the Eastern Front. *See* Guy Sajer, *The Forgotten Soldier*, (New York: Harper & Row, Publishers, Inc., 1971). Two Italian accounts are also considered to be authoritative in the descriptions of the Russian encirclement on the Don Front during the early weeks of 1943. *See* Mario Rigoni Stern, trans. Archibald Colquhoun, *The Sergeant in the Snow*, (New York: Alfred A. Knopf, 1967). *See also* Eugenio Corti, trans. Peter Edward Levy, *Few Returned: Twenty-Eight Days on the Russian Front, Winter 1942-1943*, (Columbia, MO: The University of Missouri Press, 1997) *and* Günter K. Koschorrek, *Blood Red Snow: The Memoirs of a German Soldier on the Eastern Front*, (London: Greenhill Books, 2002). The authors had discussed the foregoing works in September 2002 with the intent of

acquiring them to compare accounts. Unfortunately, Mr. Naujoks passed away on October 25, 2002, before he had the opportunity to read any of these books.

Chapter XI - A Time to Heal

[1] The RAF conducted a series of four night raids on Hamburg between July 26 and August 2, 1943. On the second raid, flown the night of July 27, the RAF employed high explosive and incendiary bombs producing the first man-made firestorm. The technique had been suggested by Air Chief Marshal Sir Arthur Tedder as a means of clearing out defensive fortifications prior to an infantry assault in the ongoing campaign against Field Marshal Rommel in North Africa. The RAF adopted it as a means of targeting civilians in Hamburg, killing over 45,000 in the July 27, 1943 raid. Firestorms were also created by the RAF at Kassel, Würzburg, Darmstadt, Heilbronn, Wuppertal, Weser and Magdeburg, by which time Air Chief Marshal Sir Arthur Harris had refined Tedder's theory for high density population centers, using high explosives to first blow out windows and collapse roofs in order to facilitate a proper draft that would create the raging inferno. This was followed by a massive attack with incendiary bombs to ignite the conflagration. The RAF attack on Dresden on February 13, 1945, a city with no significant industrial or military targets, may be the greatest single massacre in history. The RAF dropped thousands of blast bombs at first, followed by 650,000 incendiary bombs, creating a firestorm visible for 200 miles. The next day, 300 American bombers blasted the city again, attacking rail yards where thousands of refugees crowded in train cars fleeing from the Red Army advancing from the east. In the meantime, American fighter escorts strafed refugees huddled along the Elbe River. American and British officials have minimized the death count to 60,000, but the German Federal Bureau of Statistics in Wiesbaden have documented the number of deaths in excess of 600,000. The truth lies somewhere in between, though I suspect closer to the latter. *See* Piekalkiewicz, Janusz and Van Heurck, Jan. *The Air War: 1939-1945*, (Unionville, PA: Cowles Historical Society, 1986). For

an excellent account of the Dresden raid, *see also* Alexander McKee, *Dresden 1945: The Devil's Tinderbox*, (New York: Barnes & Noble Books, 2000). McKee's account was first published in 1982, and does not contain the figures later released by the German Federal Bureau of Statistics.

[2]Beevor, *Stalingrad*, 372.

[3]*Ibid.,* 381.

Chapter XII - Back to the Front

[1]Cooper, *The German Army*, 472-476.

[2]Earl Ziemke, "German-Soviet War", in Dear, *The Oxford Companion to World War II*, 445.

[3]Werth, *Russia at War*, 863.

[4]Martin Gilbert, "Final Solution", in Dear, *The Oxford Companion to World War II*, 367. *See also* Werth, *Russia at War*, 387-388.

[5] On the morning of July 13, 1944, the Red Army First Ukrainian Front began a massive offensive into Galicia as part of an overall offensive on the entire Eastern Front. By the evening of July 15, 1943, Russian tanks were within 25 miles of Lvov. *See* Ziemke, "German-Soviet War" in Dear, *The Oxford Companion to World War II*, 445.

[6]Compare to Guy Sajer, *The Forgotten Soldier,* (reprint, Washington, D.C.: Brassey's Inc., 2000) 395-396.

Chapter XIII - House of Cards

[1] Ziemke, "German-Soviet War", in Dear, *The Oxford Companion to World War II*, 447.

[2] Dear, *"Wilhelm Gustloff"*, in *The Oxford Companion to World War II*, 1273.

[3] John Toland, *The Last 100 Days*, (New York: Random House, 1966) 31-36. *See* Arthur E. Sellwood, *The Damned Don't Drown: The Sinking of the Wilhelm Gustloff*, (reprint, Annapolis, MD: Naval Institute Press, 1996). Nobel Prize winner and German author Günter Grass recently published an historical novel based on the *Wilhelm Gustloff* incident documenting several aspects of the tragedy, and underscoring the nature of unspoken suffering that befell many Germans in World War II. *See also* Gunter Grass, trans. Krishna Winston, *Crabwalk*, (New York: Harcourt, Inc, 2002).

Chapter XIV - End Game

[1] Overy, *Russia's War*, 265.

[2] Erickson, *The Road to Berlin*, 571.

[3] Overy, *Russia's War*, 263.

[4] Clare Griffiths, *Poland*, (London: Insight Guides, 1991) 321.

[5] Winston Churchill, *"Sinews of Peace"* (speech given at Westminster College in Fulton, Missouri on March 5, 1946. *See* Mark A. Kishlansky, ed., *Sources of World History*, (New York: Harper Collins, 1995) 298-302.

Chapter XV - Surrender

[1]Compare to Sajer, *The Forgotten Soldier,* 390.

[2]Joanna Egert-Romanowska and Magorzata Omilanowska, eds, *Germany* (New York: Dorling Kindersley Publishing, Inc., 2001) 456.

Chapter XVI - My Odyssey

[1]Dear, "Atlantic Charter", in *The Oxford Companion to World War II,* 69.

[2]Rodes, *Germany, A History,* 602-605.

[3]*Ibid.*

[4]*Ibid.*

[5]*Ibid.*

[6]*Ibid.,* 607-608.

[7]*Ibid.,* 602.

[8]*Ibid.,* 602-603.

[9]*Ibid.,* 610-613.

Appendix - Family Origins

[1]John E. Rodes, *Germany: A History,* (New York: Holt Rinehart and Winston, Inc., 1964) 5-9.

[2]William Urban, *The Teutonic Knights: A Military History,* (London: Greenhill Books, 2003) 11-13.

[3]*Ibid.*

[4]Rodes, *Germany: A History*, 59-60.

[5]E. Gee Nash, *The Hansa*, (reprint, New York: Barnes & Noble Books, 1995) 20-22.

[6]Richard Fletcher, *The Barbarian Conversion: From Paganism to Christianity*, (New York: Henry Holt and Company, Inc., 1998) 507.

[7]Sidney B. Fay and Klaus Epstein, *The Rise of Brandenburg-Prussia to 1786*, rev. ed. (New York: Holt Rinehart and Winston, Inc., 1964) 32-33.

[8]*Ibid.*, 33-35

[9]Ruth Leiserowitz, *Tilsit*, accessed 14 September 2002, available from http://www.lieserowitz.de/Juden/tilsitenglish.html

[10]Rodes, *Germany: A History*, 150-173.

[11]*Ibid.*, 182.

[12]Fay and Epstein, *The Rise of Brandenburg-Prussia*, 67-68.

[13]Mack Walker, *The Salzburg Transaction: Expulsion and Redemption in Eighteenth Century Germany*, (Ithaca: Cornell University Press, 1992) 74.

[14]*Ibid.*, 78.

[15]*Ibid.*, 79.

[16]This account is drawn from Max Walker's remarkable history of the dramatic events that have come to be known as *The Salzburg Transaction*. Readers seeking further information should refer to this

work set forth in footnote 12 *infra,* which is available from Cornell University Press.

[17]Walker, *The Salzburg Transaction,* 45-47.

[18]*Ibid.,* 84-85.

[19]*Ibid.,* 85-86.

[20]*Ibid.,* 88.

[21]Naujoks translated into German is Neumann.

[22]Frank McLynn, *Napoleon: A Biography,* (New York: Arcade Publishing, 2002) 356-359.

[23]*Ibid.,* 378.

[24]Rodes, *Germany: A History,* 268-271.

[25]*Ibid.,* 269.

[26]McLynn, *Napoleon,* 547, 551.

[27]Rodes, *Germany: A History,* 379.

SELECTED BIBLIOGRAPHY

Andrew, Christopher, and Vasili Mitrokhin. *The Sword and the Shield: The Mitrokhin Archive and the Secret History of he KGB.* New York: Basic Books, 1999.

Baer, Gertrude Mackprang. *In the Shadow of Silence: From Hitler Youth to Allied Internment: A Young Woman's Story of Truth and Denial.* Toronto: Harper Collins Publishers, Ltd., 2002.

Beevor, Antony. *Stalingrad: The Fateful Siege: 1942-1943.* New York: Penguin Books, 1999.

Bidermann, Gottlob Herbert. trans. Derek S. Zumbro. *In Deadly Combat: A German Soldier's Memoir of the Eastern Front.* Lawrence, KS: University Press of Kansas, 2000.

Bishop, Chris, and Adam Warner, eds. *German Campaigns of World War II.* Edison, NJ: Chartwell Books, Inc., 2001.

Bonnefoy, Yves. *Dictionnaire des Mythologies et des Religions des Sociétiés Traditionnelles et du Monde Antique.* Paris: Centre National des Lettres, 1981) trans. Wendy Doniger, as *American, African and Old European Mythologies.* Chicago: University of Chicago Press, 1993.

Brendon, Piers. *The Dark Valley: A Panorama of the 1930s.* New York: Alfred A. Knopf, 2000.

Buchner, Alex. *The German Infantry Handbook, 1939-1945.* Atglen, PA: Schiffer Publishing, Ltd., 1991.

_____. *Ostfront 1944: The German Defensive Battles on the Russian Front.* Atglen, PA: Schiffer Publishing, Ltd., 1995.

Campbell, Joseph. *The Mythic Image*. Princeton, NJ: Princeton University Press, 1974.

Cooper, Matthew. *The German Army 1933-1945*. Lanham, MD: Scarborough House, 1978.

Cornwell, John. *Hitler's Pope: The Secret History of Pius XII*. New York: Penguin Putnam, Inc., 1999.

Corti, Eugenio. trans. Peter Edward Levy. *Few Returned: Twenty-Eight Days on the Russian Front, Winter 1942-1943*. Columbia, MO: The University of Missouri Press, 1997.

Craig, William E. *Enemy at the Gates: The Battle for Stalingrad*. New York: Readers Digest Press, 1973.

_____. *Die Schlacht um Stalingrad: Der Untergang der 6. Armee Kriegswende an der Wolga*. Munich: Verlag Kurt Desch, 1974. (German version of *Enemy at the Gates*).

Cunliff, Barry, ed. *The Oxford Illustrated Prehistory of Europe*. Oxford: Oxford University Press, 1994.

Davies, Norman. *Europe: A History*. New York: Harper Collins Publishers, Inc., 1998.

Egert-Romanowska, Joanna, and Magorzata Omilanowska, ed. *Germany*. New York: Dorling Kindersley Publishing, Inc., 2001.

Ehrenburg, Ilya, trans. Tatiana Shebunina. *The War: 1941- 1945*. New York: The World Publishing Company, 1964.

Erickson, John. *The Road to Stalingrad: Stalin's War with Germany*. New Haven: Yale University Press, 1999.

_____. *The Road to Berlin: Stalin's War with Germany.* New Haven: Yale University Press, 1999.

Fay, Sydney B., and Klaus Epstein. *The Rise of Brandenburg-Prussia to 1786.* rev. ed. New York: Holt Rinehart and Winston, Inc., 1964.

Fischer, Klaus P. *Nazi Germany: A New History.* New York: Continuum Publishing Company, 1995.

Fletcher, Richard. *The Barbarian Conversion: From Paganism to Christianity.* New York: Henry Holt and Company, 1998.

Fritz, Stephen G. *Frontsoldaten: The German Soldier in World War II.* Lexington, KY: The University Press of Kentucky, 1995.

Glantz, David M., and Jonathan House. *When Titans Clashed: How The Red Army Stopped Hitler.* Lawrence, KS: The University Press of Kansas, 1995.

_____., and Helmut Heiber, eds. *Hitler and His Generals: Military Conferences 1942 - 1945.* Reprint. New York: Enigma Books, 2003.

Goldhagen, Daniel Jonah. *Hitler's Willing Executioners: Ordinary Germans and the Holocaust.* New York: Alfred A. Knopf, 1996.

Grass, Günter. trans. Krishna Winston. *Crabwalk.* New York: Harcourt, Inc. 2002.

Griffiths, Clare. *Poland.* London: Insight Guides, 1991.

Guderin, Gen. Heinz. *Panzer Leader.* Cambridge, MA: Da Capo Press, 1996.

Holmes, Blair R. and Alan F. Keele, *When Truth was Treason: German Youth Against Hitler*. Urbana, IL: University of Illinois Press, 1995.

Dear, I.C.B., ed. *The Oxford Companion to World War II*. Oxford: Oxford University Press, 1995.

Kissinger, Henry. *Diplomacy*. New York: Simon & Schuster, 1994.

Knappe, Siegfried, and Ted Brusaw. *Soldat: Reflections of a German Soldier, 1936-1949*. New York: Dell Publishing, 1992.

Koch, Hannsjoachim W. *The Hitler Youth: Origins and Development 1922-1945*. New York: Barnes & Noble Books, 1975.

Koschorrek, Günter K. *Blood Red Snow: The Memoirs of a German Soldier on the Eastern Front*. London: Greenhill Books, 2002.

Leiserowitz, Ruth. *Tilsit*, accessed 14 September 2002, available from http://www.lieserowitz.de/Juden/tilsitenglish.html

Lucas, James. *Das Reich: The Military Role of the 2nd SS Division*. Reading, Berks.: Cassell Military Paperbacks, 1999.

_____. *War on the Eastern Front: The German Soldier in Russia, 1941-1945*. Reprint. London: Greenhill Books, 1998.

Kishlansky, Mark A., ed. *Sources of World History*. New York: Harper Collins, 1995.

McCullough, David. *Truman*, New York: Simon & Schuster, 1992.

McFarland, Rick and Matt Whitaker, *Truth and Conviction*. Provo, UT: Brigham Young University, 2002. DVD Documentary Video.

McKee, Alexander. *Dresden 1945: The Devil's Tinderbox*. New York: Barnes & Noble Books, 2000.

McLynn, Frank. *Napoleon: A Biography*. New York: Arcade Publishing, 2002.

Michaels, Daniel W. "New Evidence on the 1941 'Barbarossa' Attack: Why Hitler Attacked Soviet Russia When He Did," *Journal of Historical Review*, 18 No.3 (May/June 1999) 40, reviewing Adolph von Thadden, *Stalin's Falle: Er Wollte den Kreig*, Rosenheim, DE: Kultur und Zeitgeschicte/Archiv der Zeit, 1996. Accessed 14 September 2002, available from http://www.ihr.org/ jhr/v18n3p40_Michaels.html

Mohr, Joseph. *Stille Nacht, Hielige Nacht*, ed. Marianne Mehling. Frohe Weihnacht: Geschichten, Lieder und Gedichte zur Advents und Weihnachtszeit. Munich: Droemer-Knaur, 1986.

Nash, E. Gee. *The Hansa*. Reprint. New York: Barnes & Noble Books, 1995.

Newton, Steven H. *German Battle Tactics on the Russian Front, 1941-45*. Atglen, PA: Schiffer Publishing, Ltd., 1994.

Overy, Richard. *Russia's War: A History of Russia's War Effort: 1941-1945*. New York: Penguin Books, 1998.

Parker, Sybil P., ed. *The McGraw-Hill Concise Encyclopedia of Science and Technology, 2nd Edition*. New York: McGraw-Hill Publishing Company, 1989.

Petrova, Ada, and Peter Watson. *The Death of Hitler*. New York: W.W. Norton & Company, Inc., 1995.

Piekalkiewicz, Janusz and Jan Van Heurck. *The Air War: 1939-1945*. Unionville, PA: Cowles Historical Society, 1986.

Pimlott, John. *The Historical Atlas of World War II*. New York: Henry Holt and Company, 1995.

Remak, J, ed. *The Nazi Years: A Documentary History*. Englewood Cliffs, NJ: Prentice-Hall, 1969.

Rhodes, Richard. *Masters of Death: The SS - Einsatzgruppen and the Invention of the Holocaust*. New York: Alfred A. Knopf, 2002.

Rodes, John E. *Germany: A History,* New York: Holt Rinehart and Winston, Inc., 1964.

Sajer, Guy. *The Forgotten Soldier*. New York: Harper & Row, Publishers, Inc., 1971.

Schnibbe, Karl-Heinz. *The Price: The True Story of a Mormon Who Defied Hitler*. Salt Lake City, UT: Bookcraft, Inc., 1984.

Sellwood, Arthur V. *The Damned Don't Drown: The Sinking of the Wilhelm Gustloff*. Annapolis, MD: Naval Institute Press, 1996.

Shirer, William L. *The Nightmare Years 1930-1940: A Memoir of A Life and the Times*. Boston: Little, Brown and Company, 1984.

_____. *"This is Berlin" Radio Broadcasts From Nazi Germany*. Woodstock, NY: The Overlook Press, 1999.

_____. *The Rise and Fall of the Third Reich: A History of Nazi Germany*. New York: Simon & Schuster, 1960.

Speer, Albert. *Inside the Third Reich: Memoirs.* New York: The Macmillan Company, 1970.

Stern, Mario Rigoni. trans. Archibald Colquhoun. *The Sergeant in the Snow.* New York: Alfred A. Knopf, 1967.

Tarrant, V.E. *Stalingrad: Anatomy of an Agony.* London: Leo Cooper, 1992.

Toland, John. *The Last 100 Days.* New York: Random House, 1966.

Tsouras, Peter G., ed. *Fighting in Hell: The German Ordeal on the Eastern Front.* New York: Ivy Books, 1995.

Urban, William. *The Teutonic Knights: A Military History.* London: Greenhill Books, 2003.

U.S. War Department. *Handbook on German Military Forces.* Reprint. Baton Rouge, LA: Louisiana State University Press, 1990.

U.S. War Department. *The U.S. Strategic Bombing Survey: European Theater of Operations, 2ⁿᵈ Edition.* Washington, D.C.: Government Printing Office, 1947. Accessed on 14 September 2002, available from http://www.members. tripod.com/~Sturmvogel/ussbint.html

von Clausewitz, Carl. *On War.* New York: Penguin Classics, 1982.

von Mellenthen, Maj. Gen. F.W. *Panzer Battles: A study of the Employment of Armor in the Second World War.* Norman, OK: University of Oklahoma Press, 1956.

Walker, Mack. *The Salzburg Transaction: Expulsion and Redemption in Eighteenth Century Germany.* Ithaca, NY: Cornell University Press, 1992.

Wendel, Marcus. *Third Reich Fact Book.* Accessed 14 May 2001,
    available from http://www.skalman.nu/third-reich

Werth, Alexander. *Russia at War 1941-45.* New York: Carroll &
    Graf Publishers, Inc., 1964.

Wobbe, Rudi, and Jerry Borrowman. *Three Against Hitler.* American
    Fork, UT: Covenant Communications, Inc., 1996.

Zhukov, Georgi, K. *Marshal Zhukov's Greatest Battles.* Ed. Harrison E.
    Salisbury. New York: Cooper Square Press,
    2002.

Ziemke, Earl F. *Stalingrad to Berlin: The German Defeat in the East.*
    Washington, D.C.: U.S. Army Center for Military History,
    1968.

Index

I

J

K

A Note About the Authors

Arthur O. Naujoks, Jr. was born in Tilsit, East Prussia on December 19, 1922. He served in the German Army from 1941 to 1945, earning the Iron Cross, 2nd Class. He was a missionary for the Church of Jesus Christ of Latter-day Saints in East Germany from 1945-47. He married Traudy Markgraf on October 25 1947. They fled East Germany in 1950. He worked for Radio RIAS in Berlin, the voice of Radio Free Europe, and then emigrated to the United States where he and Traudy later obtained their U.S. citizenship. Their marriage was later solemnized in the Salt Lake Temple. Art spent his career as a draftsman at Chevron Oil Company, and after retirement, he began a hobby of historical research. It culminated in the publication of his first book, *The Last Secrets of the Third Reich*. He died before his second book was published, on October 25, 2002, his 55th wedding anniversary. He was preceded in death by his wife Traudy and his daughter, Sylvia. He is survived by his son, Mario Naujoks.

Michael S. Eldredge was born July 28, 1950 in Ogden, Utah. He graduated with a B.A. in History and Political Science from Weber State College in 1971 M.A. in Political Science with a Certificate in International Relations from Utah State University in 1972; and a Juris Doctor degree from the J. Reuben Clark Law School at Brigham Young University in 1979 served six years in the U.S. Navy, including one deployment to Vietnam in 1972-73. He resigned his commission as a Lieutenant Commander. For 24 years he practiced law in the Salt Lake City area, specializing in Securities Law and Corporate Law. He began teaching at the University of Phoenix Utah Campus in 2000 He currently instructs FlexNet® classes in History. He is married to his wife Michelle; they have eight children.

and

A Note on the Type

This book was set in Garamond. The fonts are based on the fonts first cut by Claude Garamond (c. 1480-1561). Garamond was a pupil of Geoffroy Tory and is believed to have followed the Venetian models, although he introduced a number of important differences, and it is to him that we owe the letter we now know as "old style gave to his letters a certain elegance and feeling of movement that won their creator an immediate reputation and the patronage of Francis I of France.

Designed by Ray Cornia
Graphics composed by Joel Izatt
Printed and bound by BookSurge,,LLC,
Charleston, South Carolina

154234

Made in the USA